Finding Freedom

Advanced Curriculum From Vanderbilt University's Programs for Talented Youth

Finding Freedom

ELA Lessons for Gifted and Advanced Learners in Grades 6–8

Emily Mofield, Ed.D.,
& Tamra Stambaugh, Ph.D.

Routledge
Taylor & Francis Group

NEW YORK AND LONDON

First published in 2016 by Prufrock Press Inc.

Published 2021 by Routledge
605 Third Avenue, New York, NY 10017
2 Park Square, Milton Park, Abingdon, Oxon OX14 4RN

Routledge is an imprint of the Taylor & Francis Group, an informa business

Copyright © 2016 by Taylor & Francis Group

Cover design by Raquel Trevino and layout design by Allegra Denbo

ISBN 13: 978-1-0321-4387-3 (hbk)
ISBN 13: 978-1-6182-1491-1 (pbk)

DOI: 10.4324/9781003235217

Table of Contents

Dedication

To Jerry Apple, an extraordinary principal, for unlocking
my potential to grow in the field of education.

—Emily

To my nieces and nephews and other gifted students
I have worked with who need an accelerated curriculum
to stay engaged and to grow in their learning.

—Tamra

Acknowledgements

We would like to express heartfelt gratitude to the administrators and teachers who provided valuable feedback on the unit. We greatly appreciate Emilie Hall for organizing data and fine-tuning lessons during the editing process. Dr. Elizabeth Covington is appreciated for her professional insight into the development of the rhetorical analysis model to verify the scholarly validity of its use. We also wish to thank Alison Robinson for suggesting the development of a social studies model as a tool for making connections among historical ideas. Finally, we are honored to build these lessons on a solid foundation of knowledge, theory, and best practices in gifted education and curriculum development established from the inspiring work of Dr. Joyce VanTassel-Baska.

Introduction

At times, history and fate meet at a single time in a single place to
shape a turning point in man's unending search for freedom.
—Lyndon B. Johnson, 1965

Finding Freedom is designed specifically with gifted and high-achieving middle
and early high school learners in mind. These concept-based lessons are accelerated
beyond typical grade-level standards and include advanced models and organizers to help students analyze a variety of texts. This unit invites students to follow
America's journey toward finding freedom by examining multiple perspectives,
conflicts, ideas, and challenges through the analysis of primary sources and key historical events. Aligned to the Common Core State Standards (CCSS), this unit features close readings of some of the most famous American political speeches from
notable Americans, presidents, and minority voices. To sharpen historical thinking, students analyze arguments for freedom, examine dissenting perspectives,
and reason through multiple viewpoints of historical issues through debates and
interactive activities. To develop advanced literacy skills, students evaluate effective rhetorical appeals, claims, supporting evidence, and techniques that advance
arguments. Students synthesize their learning by comparing speeches to each
other, relating texts to contemporary issues of today, and making interdisciplinary
connections. Each lesson includes close readings with text-dependent questions,
choice-based differentiated products, rubrics, formative assessments, social studies
content connections, and ELA tasks that require argument and explanatory writing.
Ideal for pre-AP and honors courses, the unit features speeches from Patrick Henry,
Frederick Douglass, Carrie Chapman Catt, and Presidents Franklin D. Roosevelt,
Abraham Lincoln, John F. Kennedy, Lyndon B. Johnson, George W. Bush, Barack
Obama, and others.

DOI: 10.4324/9781003235217-1

CONCEPTUAL FRAMEWORK

Finding Freedom is one of four units designed to support the acquisition of textual analysis skills, including comprehending texts, evaluating arguments, enhancing thinking and communication skills, and connecting conceptual generalizations from cross-curricular themes to a variety of primary source documents. This particular unit focuses on linking social studies content and historical context to the understanding of primary source documents. The Integrated Curriculum Model (ICM; VanTassel-Baska, 1986) is the conceptual framework used for the unit design. Components of the framework are embedded in each lesson: accelerated content, advanced literacy processes of the discipline (e.g., rhetorical analysis), and conceptual understandings. For example, the accelerated content includes ELA (English language arts) standards, aligned to the CCSS. The CCSS selected for each unit are above the grade level(s) for which the unit was intended. Each unit also includes process skills and specific models to help students evaluate the development of effective arguments; analyze a variety of texts, art, and primary sources; and connect these to real-world events/issues (see Appendices A and B for more information on the models). The content of each lesson is connected by an overarching theme and key generalizations that span a variety of disciplines. These concepts vary by unit and include power, truth versus perception, individuality versus conformity, and freedom. Table 1 shows how each unit in this series aligns with the ICM features. The ICM model was selected based on its evidence-supported success in increasing gifted student achievement (see VanTassel-Baska & Stambaugh, 2008).

INTENDED GRADE LEVEL(S)

It is well known in gifted education that accelerated content is essential for increasing the academic achievement and social-emotional growth of gifted students (Assouline, Colangelo, VanTassel-Baska, & Lupkowski-Shoplik, 2015; Colangelo, Assouline, & Gross, 2004; Steenbergen-Hu & Moon, 2011). This unit is intended for and has been piloted with gifted students in grades 6–8. The unit is aligned to CCSS standards primarily focused on grades 9–10, with some lower grade standards included as needed. The accelerated content is necessary so that gifted students have the opportunity to gain new language arts content knowledge at a pace and level that is appropriate for their learning needs. Gifted students' readiness and experience levels vary, as do their abilities. Because school contexts and content emphases are different, it is up to each teacher to determine which unit is best suited for their particular students and at which grade levels. Some gifted stu-

Table 1

The Integrated Curriculum Model Alignment by Unit

Unit	Accelerated Content	Advanced Processes Models/Organizers	Concept/Generalizations
Finding Freedom	Aligned to grade 9 and 10 CCSS standards	Advanced Models: ■ Social Studies Connections ■ Rhetorical Analysis Organizers: ■ Reasoning About a Situation ■ Big Idea Reflection: Primary Sources	■ Freedom requires sacrifice. ■ Freedom requires responsibility. ■ Freedom is threatened by internal and external forces.
Perspectives of Power	Aligned to grade 9 and 10 CCSS standards	Advanced Models: ■ Literary Analysis ■ Visual Analysis ■ Rhetorical Analysis Organizers: ■ Big Idea Reflection ■ Reasoning About a Situation or Event	■ Power is the ability to influence. ■ Power is connected to a source. ■ Power may be used or abused.
I, Me, You, We: Individuality Versus Conformity	Aligned to grade 9 and 10 CCSS standards	Advanced Models: ■ Literary Analysis ■ Visual Analysis ■ Rhetorical Analysis Organizers: ■ Big Idea Reflection ■ Reasoning About a Situation or Event	■ Both conformity and individuality are agents of change. ■ Both conformity and individuality involve sacrifice. ■ There are positives and negatives to both conformity and individuality.
In the Mind's Eye: Truth Versus Perception	Aligned to grade 9 and 10 CCSS standards	Advanced Models: ■ Literary Analysis ■ Visual Analysis ■ Rhetorical Analysis Organizers: ■ Big Idea Reflection ■ Reasoning About a Situation or Event	■ Although truth is constant, one's perception of truth varies. ■ There are negatives and positives in realizing the truth. ■ There are consequences to believing perception rather than the truth.

4

dents may find this unit engaging as a sixth grader while others may need to wait until grade 7 or 8 to fully participate and understand the unit concepts. Teachers of 9th and 10th graders may find that these units are on target for many of their general education students.

LESSON FORMAT AND GUIDELINES

Each lesson in this unit follows a similar format for ease of use. Teachers select from a variety of questions, activities, and differentiated products to best meet their students' needs.

Alignment to Standards

The unit incorporates the key pedagogical shifts highlighted as part of the CCSS. For example, students read informational texts from a variety of sources and perspectives and work through textual analysis, as well as social studies analysis activities and questions. Through the use of primary sources, they learn domain-specific content from their readings and are required to provide text-based evidence to support their answers or ideas. Each lesson also includes opportunities for students to make or analyze an argument, defend a position, understand the context of a specific time period, and interpret a text. Of course, part of close reading and understanding a text includes the use of domain-specific vocabulary. The readings selected throughout the unit build upon specific concepts and highlight multiple perspectives. Many readings use vocabulary of the time period or a specific discipline, which students must understand and define.

The end of the unit includes a CCSS alignment sheet (p. 213). The CCSS standards are incorporated in every lesson and as such, not repeated for each lesson. This unit was not designed to meet every CCSS ELA standard for a particular grade level.

Materials

When differentiating for the gifted, it is important for the materials and readings to be at a level commensurate with the student's ability. The readings and resources in this unit have been carefully selected and include either sophisticated concepts or reading selections above most middle school grade levels. The materials section includes a list of resources needed for the lesson. Some of the listed materials are optional and many of the selected texts, visuals, or videos are readily available online as a free download. When possible, reliable sites and specific links, available at the time of this unit's printing, are provided. *A word of caution*: It is important to note that some of the readings may be controversial or contain advanced or sensitive concepts and content. A cautionary note is provided in lessons with the most controversial issues. Still, it is up to the teacher and school administration to understand the context of his or her district and to determine whether or not a reading or discussion is appropriate or whether a different text or discussion-based question should be used. As the lessons follow a specific format and the analysis models can be used with any text, teachers may easily substitute a more appropriate source and then apply questions and activities for that source using a selected analysis model as a guide (see Appendix A for specific descriptions of each model).

Introductory Activities

The introductory activities provide a real-world connection or "hook" that sets the tone for the remainder of the lesson and enhances student engagement. Sample options include quick debates about an issue or dilemma, symbol designs to illustrate a key concept or idea, or key discussion questions that help students better understand the relevance of a lesson's text.

Text-Dependent Questions for Close Reading

This section provides questions that ensure students understand the text. These close reading questions are varied and the majority focus on comprehension and inference making. Students are to answer these questions using textual evidence. Note that prediction or speculation questions that cannot be supported with evidence from the text are not appropriate for this section. A variety of questions are listed, but not all questions should be asked in a given lesson. Instead, teachers select four to six questions from the list for students to discuss in small groups, Socratic seminars, or as an entire class. Of course, if students are struggling to understand the text, additional questions or background information may be required. The questions in this section are *not* intended as homework or to be responded to in writing on a consistent basis. These questions are designed for discussion purposes so that teachers can check for understanding and help students support new ideas or clarify misunderstandings.

Analysis Section

This is the most comprehensive and complex section of each lesson and includes a rhetorical analysis model to help students identify and analyze rhetorical arguments given the selected primary sources. See Appendix A for a detailed explanation, instructions, and an example lesson and Appendix B for blank copies of the model and a guide.

It is important to note that the rhetorical analysis model is used in every lesson. Teachers may choose to use this analysis model each time they teach a lesson or simply refer to it for certain lessons without completing a full analysis. If the latter is chosen, teachers would focus more on another section of the unit, such as big ideas and real-world connections, concepts, or differentiated products.

In-Class Activities to Deepen Learning

The activities included here provide hands-on or thought-provoking ideas that support or solidify student learning. Tasks incorporate real-world connections and include issue-based questions linked to a big idea, quick debates about a controversial issue, or technology extensions. These activities also include opportunities for self-reflection on how the lesson content impacted their learning. One or all of the activities in this section may be taught.

Concept Connections

The concept connections section focuses on the third component of the ICM. The purpose of this section is to help students see the relationships between different texts and perspectives as these relate to key generalizations about freedom. A graphic organizer comprised of the conceptual generalizations and key unit readings is provided in the unit to help students organize their ideas and determine patterns among the various readings. It is important to refer to the concept generalizations in each lesson, even if the concept chart is not completed for every reading.

Choice-Based Differentiated Products

Several choice-based differentiated products are also part of each lesson. Students may select one of the choice products to showcase their strengths and individual understanding or, if pressed for time, teachers may require two or three choice-based products for students to complete during the course of the unit. The options listed allow students an opportunity to pursue their interests and to gain a deeper understanding of a learning objective as they present their understanding in a creative way. Differentiated products vary by lesson and may include investigating a real-world problem, designing visuals, applying an advanced model to other related sources, writing essays, and developing products or presentations for an audience. Rubrics are provided in Appendix C to guide product creation and teacher feedback. The rubrics may also be used for peer and self-evaluations.

ELA Practice Tasks

Designed with the CCSS assessments in mind, the ELA practice tasks support the writing and argument analysis items typically assessed as part of a state assessment. The ELA tasks incorporate multiple standards and require complex thinking. Students are asked to respond to a prompt by creating a well-developed essay in which they create or analyze arguments, critique texts, explain an issue from multiple perspectives, or determine key concepts presented in a text. It is at the teacher's discretion to determine how many ELA practice tasks students should write throughout the course of the unit. Although not explicitly stated in the unit, teachers are encouraged to model the writing process, help students analyze exemplars and inappropriate responses, and provide individual feedback.

Social Studies Connections

The social studies connections examples, unique to this unit, include content-based and text-based questions to help students understand the various influences of the period as well as the intent of the primary source document. Each question is labeled as text- or content-dependent. Background knowledge in social studies is assumed but may need to be taught if students have not yet studied specific historical events or time periods. A social studies connection wheel (see Appendix A for instructions) and big idea reflection guide for primary sources (see Appendix B) are also a key feature in this section. These tools can be used to help students analyze key ideas of a primary source and to understand the influences and interactions that led to an event.

Formative Assessment

The formative assessment section focuses on assessing a student's understanding of a single-faceted objective, such as making inferences or determining how an author crafted an argument. A rubric is included with each prompt so that teachers can quickly assess responses, provide feedback, and determine next steps in their students' learning. Questions require a written response of no more than a paragraph. The formative assessments may be used to determine the extent to which students understand the meaning of a text and can provide supporting evidence and target instruction based on individual needs. Teachers may require students to complete an ELA practice task in one lesson and a formative assessment task in another so that students' thinking and understanding can be measured in a variety of ways.

Handouts

Following each lesson, all necessary handouts for lesson completion are included (e.g., readings, organizers, blank analysis models, and other sources not readily available online). As previously stated in the materials section, sometimes teachers are led to specific web-based links, or it is recommended that popular sources be found online. This is especially important for popularized primary sources and texts. Any source that is essential to the lesson or is difficult to access is included as a handout.

Other Unit Features

This unit includes a culminating lesson that synthesizes many of the learning objectives into a comprehensive project so that students may showcase their learning in a creative way. These options may include the application of the advanced content learned throughout the unit, real-world problem solving, and the development of authentic products. Additionally, the culminating lesson includes in-depth self-reflections that guide students to relate their own lives to concept themes. Rubrics are provided so that students understand the expectations of a task and teachers can easily analyze student products given set criteria. The rubrics are also useful for peer and self-evaluations.

Teacher background information is another feature of many lessons, especially those with more complicated texts. Although some background information is provided, teachers are encouraged to research the history of a specific primary source (if not already known) and seek varied interpretations of the text.

Sample responses are also included for many complex questions and analysis models. It is important to understand that the answers provided are a guide and should not be construed as the only correct response. Student answers will vary and many unanticipated responses may be correct. Teachers are encouraged to use the provided sample responses to better understand the intent of the question, to model how to arrive at an appropriate response, to model how to use a specific analysis tool, or to familiarize themselves with the intent of a particular passage.

Finally, this unit features instructions for using models, sample model lessons, blank model handouts, and guides to support students' thinking about each element of a given analysis model. Rubrics are also provided to assess student products and responses. Specifically, Appendix A highlights instructions, handouts, and examples for each analysis model. Appendix B includes blank models and guides for thinking about each element of a particular model, and Appendix C includes rubrics for assessing student progress.

Time Allotment

Most lessons can be taught within 90–120 minutes, though some lessons may take longer. The length of the lesson also depends upon how many models and activities are employed, how interested students are in a particular issue or text, and how many times a text needs to be read or analyzed for students to gain understanding. In general, it is anticipated that this unit can be taught with approximately 45 hours of instruction time if teachers follow the recommended guidelines as reported in this section.

Differentiation

Gifted students are a heterogeneous group and their ability levels, pace of learning, interests, and depth of understanding vary. Although this unit was written with gifted middle school students in mind, differentiation is still necessary. A variety of differentiated opportunities are embedded in the unit, such as choice-based product options, open-ended questions, and more simple and complex ways to adapt the analysis models and adjust instruction based on students' readiness and interest levels.

The "choice-based differentiated products" section in each lesson allows students to select a task of interest and to showcase their learning in a way that best meets their individual preferences and learning styles. In addition, the final lesson synthesizes unit goals and provides opportunities for students to select a project of their own choosing to explore in depth. The close reading questions can also be differentiated. Teachers may assign specific questions to individual students or groups of students based on their responses from formative assessments or ELA tasks.

The process models (e.g., rhetorical analysis, social studies connections, and big idea) are easily differentiated as well. For example, the rhetorical analysis wheel and social studies connections wheel automatically provide a framework for teachers to ask simple questions using only one element, or more complex questions by emphasizing relationships among various elements (e.g., how the economic conditions of the day influenced the concept of equity or how an author's style was used to evoke emotion). Likewise, students who need more practice understanding a text may use the simpler text-based model (in Appendix B) instead of the rhetorical analysis model. The teacher may also differentiate the in-class activities by assigning different groups of students to specific tasks. These can be designed as differentiated stations. Of course, not all students would complete work at every station, but would be assigned a station based on their readiness. After the complexity of the task is established, then activities, questions, or product choices may also be included to accommodate various learning styles or interests.

The positive academic effects of grouping gifted students and accelerating the content they are taught are well documented (see the meta analyses of Kulik & Kulik, 1992, and Rogers, 2007). However, not all middle schools are designed to support accelerated courses for their high-achieving students. Experienced teachers of general classrooms may use this unit with their gifted and high-achieving students as part of a deliberate differentiated approach that includes in-class flexible groupings and tiered questions, stations, and assignments.

Multicultural Connections

Efforts were made to include sources that showcase a variety of authors from varying ethnicities, perspectives, and genders. Activities and readings encourage conversations about equity, civil rights, and other key issues as they relate to freedom. Teachers may substitute certain readings or adjust questions and discussions based on their specific school population and local community culture.

Assessment and Grading

Formative, diagnostic-prescriptive, and summative performance-based assessments are an essential part of the unit. Assessment data come from a variety of sources and are used to monitor student growth, provide student feedback, allow for student self-reflection, or to differentiate content or instruction. Descriptions of the assessments used in this unit are as follows:

- **Diagnostic-prescriptive assessment:** The unit pretest provides a first glimpse of a student's current level of performance. Each question focuses on a different key understanding. For example, Questions 1 and 2 focus on the relationship between different rhetorical elements, Question 3 focuses on making inferences and providing evidence, and Question 4 focuses on concepts or themes. Reponses for each question can be used to differentiate questions for different groups of students and to assign specific tasks that support student learning in a key area. Prior to Lesson 1, administer the pretest (p. 14) and use the rubric (p. 17) to score responses. See Appendix A (p. 185) for a sample analysis of the pretest text, which can be used to introduce rhetorical elements after the pretest.
- **Formative assessment:** There are many opportunities throughout the unit for teachers to check for student understanding. Teachers may occasionally ask students to expand, in writing, upon their answer to an assigned question from the text-dependent questions of a particular lesson so that comprehension can be assessed. A rubric is provided as part of the Formative Assessment section in each lesson to check for understanding. This rubric can also be used to monitor student growth and to provide feedback.

The ELA Practice Tasks and Formative Assessment sections may also be assigned and graded to determine the level of student understanding as well as misconceptions about specific sources or texts that may need reteaching or further exploration. It is not recommended that every lesson's formative assessment or ELA task be assigned or graded, although teachers may select two or three of each throughout the course of the unit to use for this purpose. Informally, teachers may gather formative assessment data by listening to student discussions to ensure that students understand the text. Differentiated choice products may also be used as a formative assessment and graded using the provided rubric. Teachers should encourage students to engage in self-reflection as they receive feedback from a variety of assessments.

- **Summative assessment:** There are two different summative assessments in the unit. The final lesson (Lesson 12) includes culminating choice-based products for students to showcase their understanding of key unit content, processes, and concepts through selected product-creations. In addition, the postassessment of the unit can also be used as a summative assessment and also to measure student growth, when compared with the preassessment.

Appendix C includes rubrics for the various product-based assessments, which can also be used for peer and self-evaluations. Rubrics for the pre- and postassessments are included with the appropriate assessment at the beginning or end of the unit.

MAKING THE MOST OUT OF THE UNIT

The following ideas are important to consider before teaching the unit:
- Provide professional development about the units that includes both content and pedagogy. Some of the unit content is complex and background knowledge may be needed. Read Appendix A instructions and examples for using the analysis models before teaching the unit. Practice completing the models on your own using specific texts before asking the students to do so until you understand how the models are used.
- For those students who need more scaffolding, consider teaching the models separately first with easier texts to get students accustomed to different ways of thinking before adding complex resources, issues, and concepts.
- You may need to teach the individual elements of each analysis model before combining them. Because gifted students learn at a faster pace, teaching individual elements can be done more quickly so that you can focus on

depth and complexity through the relationships between the different elements. (This concept applies to each of the models.)

- Ensure that each individual lesson incorporates advanced content, an analysis model (e.g., rhetorical), and links to the concept generalizations, as these are critical components of the ICM framework.
- Read the texts and prompts ahead of time to make sure the selections are appropriate for your district context. Substitute readings and visuals as appropriate.
- Make sure the online resources and YouTube videos are still available before teaching a particular lesson.
- Follow your students. Sometimes a lesson or reading may prompt important discussions that continue beyond the allotted time period.
- Know the intent of the models and the lesson outcomes so that you can best guide students toward important process, content, and concept goals. Otherwise, the issues discussed may supersede the objectives, especially with passionate gifted students.
- Don't assign text-dependent questions as in-depth writing activities or homework as the norm. Discussion and teacher feedback are important and most of the questions in the unit are intended to be part of a small- or whole-group discussion. By engaging students through group discussions, you can correct misconceptions right away and solicit multiple perspectives and ideas that can enhance student learning.
- Be sure to emphasize the use of supporting evidence and the complex relationships among various elements of a model when facilitating student discussions.
- Have fun! We have enjoyed teaching these units and listening to teacher feedback. We hope these units not only show academic gains in your students, but also encourage them to become citizens who can critically analyze situations and enact positive change.

UNIT GOALS AND OBJECTIVES

Content

Goal 1: To analyze and interpret primary source texts. Students will be able to:
- explain with evidence how a writer develops and supports a claim,
- respond to interpretations of historical speeches through a variety of contexts,

- compare and contrast various texts and real-world events on themes and generalizations, and
- evaluate rhetorical devices that influence effective argumentation within primary source documents.

Process

Goal 2: To develop thinking, writing, and communication skills in the language arts. Students will be able to:

- reason through an issue by combining a variety of reasoning strategies (i.e., determine implications and consequences, consider multiple points of view, examine assumptions behind multiple points of view, inferring from data);
- use evidence to develop appropriate inferences;
- evaluate the use of effective argumentation given a specific model;
- analyze primary sources by determining purposes, assumptions, and consequences of primary sources within a historical context; and
- analyze societal or individual conflicts resulting from the struggle for freedom.

Concept

Goal 3: To explain how the theme of *freedom* and related generalizations are evident given specific prompts. Students will be able to:

- support freedom generalizations with evidence from texts;
- apply inductive reasoning to develop generalizations relating to the concepts of freedom, security, individuals, diversity, equality, and democracy;
- describe external and internal threats to personal and national freedom; and
- explain definitions of freedom, means and motives for achieving freedom, and implications for freedom.

Pretest

"Second Inaugural Address" *by Franklin D. Roosevelt*

Directions: Please read the passage and answer the questions thoroughly and thoughtfully. Be sure to provide evidence to support your answer. After reading, complete the questions within 30 minutes.

Delivered January 20, 1937

. . . Among men of good will, science and democracy together offer an ever-richer life and ever-larger satisfaction to the individual. With this change in our moral climate and our rediscovered ability to improve our economic order, we have set our feet upon the road of enduring progress.

Shall we pause now and turn our back upon the road that lies ahead? Shall we call this the promised land? Or, shall we continue on our way? For "each age is a dream that is dying, or one that is coming to birth."

Many voices are heard as we face a great decision. Comfort says, "Tarry a while." Opportunism says, "This is a good spot." Timidity asks, "How difficult is the road ahead?"

True, we have come far from the days of stagnation and despair. Vitality has been preserved. Courage and confidence have been restored. Mental and moral horizons have been extended.

But our present gains were won under the pressure of more than ordinary circumstances. Advance became imperative under the goad of fear and suffering. The times were on the side of progress.

To hold to progress today, however, is more difficult. Dulled conscience, irresponsibility, and ruthless self-interest already reappear. Such symptoms of prosperity may become portents of disaster! Prosperity already tests the persistence of our progressive purpose.

Let us ask again: Have we reached the goal of our vision of that fourth day of March 1933? Have we found our happy valley?

I see a great nation, upon a great continent, blessed with a great wealth of natural resources. Its hundred and thirty million people are at peace among themselves; they are making their country a good neighbor among the nations. I see a United States which can demonstrate that, under democratic methods of government, national wealth can be translated into a spreading volume of human comforts hitherto unknown, and the lowest standard of living can be raised far above the level of mere subsistence.

But here is the challenge to our democracy: In this nation I see tens of millions of its citizens—a substantial part of its whole population—who at this very moment are denied the greater part of what the very lowest standards of today call the necessities of life.

I see millions of families trying to live on incomes so meager that the pall of family disaster hangs over them day by day.

DOI: 10.4324/9781003235217-2

Pretest, Continued
_____

I see millions whose daily lives in city and on farm continue under conditions labeled indecent by a so-called polite society half a century ago.

I see millions denied education, recreation, and the opportunity to better their lot and the lot of their children.

I see millions lacking the means to buy the products of farm and factory and by their poverty denying work and productiveness to many other millions.

I see one-third of a nation ill-housed, ill-clad, ill-nourished.

But it is not in despair that I paint you that picture. I paint it for you in hope—because the nation, seeing and understanding the injustice in it, proposes to paint it out. We are determined to make every American citizen the subject of his country's interest and concern; and we will never regard any faithful law-abiding group within our borders as superfluous. The test of our progress is not whether we add more to the abundance of those who have much; it is whether we provide enough for those who have too little.

If I know aught of the spirit and purpose of our Nation, we will not listen to comfort, opportunism, and timidity. We will carry on.

Overwhelmingly, we of the Republic are men and women of good will; men and women who have more than warm hearts of dedication; men and women who have cool heads and willing hands of practical purpose as well. They will insist that every agency of popular government use effective instruments to carry out their will.

Government is competent when all who compose it work as trustees for the whole people. It can make constant progress when it keeps abreast of all the facts. It can obtain justified support and legitimate criticism when the people receive true information of all that government does.

If I know aught of the will of our people, they will demand that these conditions of effective government shall be created and maintained. They will demand a nation uncorrupted by cancers of injustice and, therefore, strong among the nations in its example of the will to peace.

Today we reconsecrate our country to long-cherished ideals in a suddenly changed civilization. In every land there are always at work forces that drive men apart and forces that draw men together. In our personal ambitions we are individualists. But in our seeking for economic and political progress as a nation, we all go up, or else we all go down, as one people.

QUESTIONS

1. What is Roosevelt's main claim and how is it supported? Provide textual evidence.

2. How effective is Roosevelt in developing his argument? Support your answer by referring to elements of effective argumentation.

3. What can you infer is meant by the phrase, "Prosperity already tests the persistence of our progressive purpose," and how does it relate to the societal conflict addressed?

4. What does this passage reveal about the big idea of freedom? Support your answer with textual evidence.

Pretest Rubric

"Second Inaugural Address" *by Franklin D. Roosevelt*

	0	1	2	3	4
Question 1: Content: Claim and Evidence	Provides no response.	Response is limited, vague, and/or inaccurate. Only the claim is mentioned with little support.	Response lacks adequate explanation. Some parts of the response are correct, but the response only vaguely addresses the author's claim and evidence. Response lacks support.	Response is accurate and makes sense. Response includes one to two examples of support for the claim.	Response is accurate, insightful, and well written. Response includes two to three examples of support for the claim with textual evidence.
Question 2: Content: Effective Rhetoric	Provides no response.	Response is limited and vague. Response only partially answers the question. A rhetorical elements is not mentioned or is merely named with no example from text.	Response is accurate with one to two rhetorical elements mentioned. Response includes limited or no evidence from text.	Response is appropriate and accurate, describing at least two rhetorical elements to support effective argumentation. Response includes some evidence from the text.	Response is insightful and well supported, describing at least three rhetorical elements. Response includes substantial evidence from the text.
Question 3: Inference From Evidence	Provides no response.	Response is limited, vague, and/or inaccurate. There is no justification for answers given.	Response is accurate, but lacks adequate explanation. Response includes some justification about the societal conflict.	Response is accurate and makes sense. Response includes some justification about the societal conflict.	Response is accurate, insightful, interpretive, and well written. Response includes thoughtful justification about the societal conflict.
Question 4: Concept/Theme	Provides no response.	Response is limited, vague, and/or inaccurate.	Response lacks adequate explanation. Response does not relate or create a generalization about freedom. Little or no evidence from text.	Response is accurate and makes sense. Response relates to or creates an idea about freedom with some relation to the text.	Response is accurate, insightful, and well written. Response relates to or creates a generalization about freedom with evidence from the text.

Note: See p. 185 (Appendix A) for a sample analysis of this text.

Finding Freedom © Taylor & Francis   DOI: 10.4324/9781003235217-3

Lesson

1

"Give Me Liberty or Give Me Death"
by Patrick Henry

Goals/Objectives

Content: To analyze and interpret primary source texts, students will be able to:

- explain with evidence how a writer develops and supports a claim,
- respond to interpretations of historical speeches through a variety of contexts,
- compare and contrast various texts and real-world events on themes and generalizations, and
- evaluate rhetorical devices that influence effective argumentation within primary source documents.

Process: To develop thinking, writing, and communication, students will be able to:

- reason through an issue by analyzing points of view, assumptions, and implications;
- use evidence to develop appropriate inferences;
- evaluate use of effective argumentation;
- analyze primary sources (purpose, assumptions, consequences); and
- analyze societal or individual conflicts resulting from the struggle for freedom.

Concept: To understand the theme of freedom and related generalizations, students will be able to:

- support freedom generalizations with evidence from texts;
- apply inductive reasoning to develop generalizations relating to the concepts of freedom, security, individuals, diversity, equality, and democracy;
- describe external and internal threats to personal and national freedom; and
- examine definitions of freedom, means and motives for achieving freedom, and implications for freedom.

 DOI: 10.4324/9781003235217-4

Materials

- Student copies of "Shall Liberty or Empire Be Sought," available online at http://www.lexrex.com/enlightened/writings/liberty_empire.htm
- Handout 1.1: "Give Me Liberty or Give Me Death" by Patrick Henry
- Handout 1.2: Blank Rhetorical Analysis Wheel
- Handout 1.3: Reasoning About a Situation or Event
- Rubric 1: Product Rubric (Appendix C)

Introductory Activities

1. Explain to students that this unit explores the concept of freedom as it has evolved over the course of American history. Ask students: *How do you define freedom?*

2. In groups of three to four, ask students to draw symbols for freedom. Have students share their drawings. As students share, bring students' attention to personal freedoms of U.S. citizens. Discuss the U.S. Constitution and its amendments if students did not include some of these freedoms within their definitions or drawings (e.g., freedom of press, speech, religion, right to bear arms, right to vote, etc.).

3. Assign the following quotes to groups of students. Students will draw an illustration of the quote and explain to the class what the quote means.
   - "Liberty means responsibility. That is why most men dread it."—George Bernard Shaw
   - "You can't separate peace from freedom because no one can be at peace unless he has his freedom."—Malcolm X
   - "I would rather be exposed to the inconveniences attending too much liberty than to those attending too small a degree of it."—Thomas Jefferson
   - "The love of liberty is the love of others; the love of power is the love of ourselves."—William Hazlitt
   - "They who can give up essential liberty to obtain a little temporary safety deserve neither liberty nor safety."—Benjamin Franklin
   - "Those who deny freedom to others deserve it not for themselves."—Abraham Lincoln
   - "Nothing, everything, anything, something: If you have nothing, then you have everything, because you have the freedom to do anything, without the fear of losing something."—Jarod Kintz
   - "I predict future happiness for Americans, if they can prevent the government from wasting the labors of the people under the pretense of taking care of them."—Thomas Jefferson

- "When the people fear the government there is tyranny, when the government fears the people there is liberty."—Thomas Jefferson
- "None are more hopelessly enslaved than those who falsely believe they are free."—Johann Wolfgang von Goethe

4. Give brief background information about the Revolutionary War and Patrick Henry. Present this as "Fact or Fiction." Ask students to stand on opposite sides of the room if they believe the following statements are "fact" or "fiction." Use this activity as a preassessment of what students already know about Patrick Henry and to teach important background information about the context of his life and speech.

- Patrick Henry is considered a Founding Father of the United States. (Fact: He is considered a Founding Father because he participated in winning American Independence. The seven *key* Founding Fathers, however, are George Washington, Thomas Jefferson, Alexander Hamilton, Benjamin Franklin, John Jay, James Madison, and John Adams.)
- Patrick Henry was the governor of Virginia twice. (Fact: He was the first and sixth governor of postcolonial Virginia.)
- Patrick Henry was opposed to the adoption of the United States Constitution. (Fact: He felt that the Constitution was a threat to individual's rights and freedoms. He thought the presidency could become a monarchy.)
- Patrick Henry is famous for his "Join or Die" propaganda cartoon. (Fiction: Benjamin Franklin is famous for this propaganda; Patrick Henry is remembered for his speech, "Give Me Liberty or Give Me Death.")
- Patrick Henry was a plantation owner with 70–80 slaves. (Fact: Patrick Henry owned a 10,000-acre farm in Virginia.)
- Patrick Henry was a prominent lawyer in Virginia. (Fact: After being unsuccessful as a farmer and business owner, he practiced law.)
- Patrick Henry participated in the Boston Tea Party. (Fiction: Patrick Henry's anti-British action was against the Stamp Act. Patrick Henry served in the Virginia House of Burgesses, the legislature of the Virginia colony. He introduced a resolution opposing the Stamp Act of 1765. His speech to the House of Burgesses was considered almost treason because it brought to surface the idea of taxation without representation. He apologized after giving a speech about the resolution and assured the House of his loyalty to the king. Ten years later, however, he renounced his loyalty.)
- Patrick Henry did not fight in the Revolutionary War. (Fiction: He was a colonel of the 1st Virginia Regiment and was involved in the famous "Gunpowder Incident.")

- Patrick Henry's famous "Give Me Liberty or Give Me Death" speech was presented to the British monarchy. (Fiction: His famous speech was delivered in 1775 to the House of Burgesses to persuade the rallying of troops against British troops. Note that this was given 10 years after the Stamp Act Resolution speech, for which he apologized.)
- Patrick Henry's wife had a mental illness and was thought to have been "possessed by the devil." (Fact: Sarah, Patrick Henry's wife, did suffer from a mental condition and was dangerous to herself and others. She was denied a Christian funeral and burial when she died. They had six children.)

Text-Dependent Questions

1. Distribute Handout 1.1: "Give Me Liberty or Give Me Death" by Patrick Henry.
2. Remind students that this was delivered to the House of Burgesses (the colonial Virginia legislature) to persuade the mobilization of troops against British troops. "President" in the speech refers to President of the House of Burgesses.
3. Allow students to read the text individually first to understand Henry's central ideas; then, read a paragraph at a time aloud, selecting from the following text-dependent questions as a guide or as part of a Socratic seminar:
   - Reread the first paragraph. Why is knowing the truth better than believing an illusion?
   - Why does Henry use the allusion of "the siren"? What effect does it have on his message?
   - According to Henry, why can't the British be trusted?
   - What does Henry mean by the allusion "betray with a kiss"? What is his desired effect in using this allusion?
   - When Henry says, "Let us not deceive ourselves," to what is he referring?
   - According to Henry, what is Britain's motive?
   - Does Henry provide adequate evidence that all options besides war have been exhausted? Explain your answer by referring to the text.
   - How does Henry support the claim that the colonists have done all they could do to "avert the storm"? How does he structure this evidence? (Sample response: It's structured through cause-effect statements.)
   - Henry makes the claim, "We must fight." Examine the number of "if" statements used to support this claim. Which "if" statement is most powerful?
   - What is meant by the phrase, "Is life so dear, or peace so sweet, as to be purchased at the price of chains and slavery?" What literary technique is

he using and what is his desired effect? (Sample response: Metaphor—Henry makes a comparison.)

- Henry uses both "I" and "we" pronouns when referring to his audience. When and why does he use these pronouns? What effect do these pronouns produce on the audience? Why does he end with "Give me liberty or give me death" instead of "Give us liberty or give us death"?
- On what points do you think Henry and the audience agree? On what points do they disagree? How can you support your inferences?
- To what extent does Henry's reasoning and evidence support his claim?
- What parts of the text are most moving and patriotic? Why?

Rhetorical Analysis

1. Briefly explain Aristotle's Elements of Rhetoric. Aristotle's rhetoric includes logos, ethos, and pathos appeals. This enhances a writer's ability to persuade an audience. (See Appendix A for more information and examples, and Handout 1.2 for a copy of the Blank Rhetorical Analysis Wheel.)
   - **Logos:** How the author establishes good reasoning to make the document/speech make sense. This includes major points, use of evidence, syllogisms, examples, evidence, facts, statistics, etc. Text-focused.
   - **Ethos:** How the author develops credibility and trust. Author-focused.
   - **Pathos:** How the author appeals to the audience's emotion. Audience-focused.

2. Review a few techniques students may see in documents; some examples are listed below (see Appendix A for a more thorough list). The teacher may choose to focus on a few techniques rather than all. The following are especially important in Henry's speech:
   - **Language:** Consider how world choice affects tone.
   - **Positive and negative connotations of words:** Consider how words evoke feelings.
   - **Allusion:** A reference to a historical or biblical work, person, or event; the writer assumes the reader can make connections between the allusion and text being read.
   - **Rhetorical question:** A question asked by the writer but that is not expected to be answered aloud; evokes reflection.
   - **Liberty rhetoric:** Using patriotic appeals for freedom.

3. Explain to students that they will now look at how Patrick Henry used these elements in his speech. Students will see how his point of view, techniques,

and organization of the speech were used to develop logos, ethos, and pathos appeals. Together, these elements develop his main claim.

4. Using Handout 1.2: Blank Rhetorical Analysis Wheel, guide students in understanding how Patrick Henry used effective argumentation techniques. Students think about the rhetorical situation (e.g., purpose, context, audience), means of persuasion (e.g., ethos, logos, and pathos appeals), and rhetorical strategies (e.g., techniques, evidence, structure/organization, etc.). Emphasize specific elements first (e.g., logos, pathos, ethos, organization, techniques, and point of view), then move toward combining elements for more complexity (e.g., what techniques does he use to develop pathos appeals?). Note that the inner wheel conceptually spins so that elements interact with the outer wheel. Refer to Appendix A for detailed instructions about the Rhetorical Analysis Wheel and how to make a hands-on model.

5. The Rhetorical Analysis Wheel Guide (Appendix B) shows specific prompts to guide students in thinking through each separate element. They may take notes on the Blank Rhetorical Analysis Wheel using arrows to show how elements relate. It is suggested that students first note the answers to each element separately on the graphic organizer, and then discuss their interactions. Consider making a poster of the Rhetorical Analysis Wheel Guide to refer to throughout the unit. For a simpler version of this model, see the Text Analysis Wheel in Appendix B. Instead of focusing on the rhetorical appeals (logos, ethos, and pathos) to support a claim, this model focuses on why the author chose to use specific points to advance a central idea. The Text Analysis Wheel may be used as scaffolding for those students who need more guidance in understanding how to interpret text.

6. *Note*: Throughout the unit, students will feel more familiar with applying the rhetorical analysis to text. Consider exposing them to specific parts of the model at first and then, over time, exposing more elements. For example, you may wish to first emphasize how techniques are used to develop appeals and focus on structure in later lessons. Over the course of the unit, emphasize how all of the elements work together to develop the main claim or central idea. Some sample questions and responses to lead the analysis include:

   ■ **Context/Purpose:**
      - *What is the historical context?* Henry's famous speech was delivered in 1775 to the House of Burgesses (the colonial legislature) to persuade the mobilizing against British troops. *Note*: "Mr. President" is not anyone in Britain or the president of the United States (some students may assume he is). "Mr. President" is the president of the Virginia legislature.
      - *What is Henry's purpose?* His goal is to develop an argument for fighting against the British.

- **Claim:**
  - *What is Henry's main claim?* We must fight because all other efforts have been exhausted.

- **Point of View/Assumptions:**
  - *What are Henry's assumptions?* He assumes that fighting is the only option left.

- **Logos/Techniques/Structure:**
  - *How does Henry present his main points? What techniques are used? How does he organize his reasoning?*
    - **Logos/Reasoning:** He presents a question (Do we want freedom or slavery?), discusses the lack of real truth, points out examples of war preparations from the British and the colonists' attempts for peace, and explains why war is inevitable.
    - **Techniques:** He presents a stark contrast in the opening question, an allusion to the "siren" to illustrate that colonists have been misled, appeal to logic ("I know of no way of judging the future but by the past"), use of rhetorical questions to emphasize points, use of parallelism ("If we wish to be free . . . "), examples of Britain's preparations for war and the colonists' attempts at peace, repetition of the main claim ("We must fight!"), use of evidence ("three millions of people" are able to fight), and an appeal to religion ("God will help bring us to destiny").
    - **Structure:** Inductive. He uses evidence throughout his speech to build his claim at the end of the third paragraph ("We must fight!").

- **Pathos/Techniques/Structure:**
  - *How does Henry develop emotional appeals?* He uses rhetorical questions to prompt audience reflection, uses positive and negative loaded language throughout (e.g., "war," "subjugation," "submission," "vigilant," "brave," etc.), and ends with exclamatory phrases to evoke excitement and patriotism.

- **Ethos/Techniques/Structure:**
  - *How does Henry develop credibility and trust?* He acknowledges that he doesn't want to be disrespectful but speaks freely, recognizes the opposing side, and uses "us" and "we" to include himself in the efforts made and to establish a personal connection with the audi-

ence. At the end, he refers to "me and I" to state his personal bravery in defending his claim, even unto death.

- ■ **Implications:**
  - *What are the implications/consequences of this document?* This speech influenced the Revolutionary War.

- ■ **Evaluation:**
  - *How effective is the author in supporting his claim? Is there a balance of pathos, ethos, and logos appeals? Is there too much bias or emotional manipulation? Is the claim fully supported?* The speech adequately supports the claim with a balance of appeals (cite evidence). He may show some bias in his point of view and emphatic appeals, but overall, this does not take away from the credibility.

In-Class Activity to Deepen Learning

Using Handout 1.3: Reasoning About a Situation or Event, students will address the question, "Should the colonists support Patrick Henry's ideas?" Explain the following concepts to students (Figure 1.1 provides some possible student responses):
- ■ *Stakeholders*: Loyalists, Patriots, British.
- ■ *Point of view* includes how the stakeholder(s) would answer the question, including evidence of why they would feel this way.
- ■ *Assumptions* are the values and beliefs taken for granted by the stakeholders.
- ■ *Implications* are the short- and long-term consequences that happened or could have happened if that particular point of view were actualized.

For additional insight, students may read a primary source document from a Loyalist perspective from the Library of Congress (e.g., Joseph Galloway's speech to Continental Congress, September 28, 1774, available at: http://www.loc.gov/teachers/classroommaterials/presentationsandactivities/presentations/timeline/amrev/rebelln/galloway.html).

Concept Connections

1. Explain to students that during the unit, they will be looking at specific concepts related to the theme of Freedom. Ask: *What general statements can we say about freedom? We will call these statements "generalizations" because we can take an idea from a specific text and generalize it to the broader world. We will look at ideas from the lesson and think about how they fit together to*

	Loyalists	Patriots	British
Point of View	No. We should be loyal to the British crown.	Yes. We have to take a stand against the unfair British rule.	No. We have a right to dominate and govern the colonies.
Assumptions	There is freedom under the rule of British government; life is not that bad.	Under the oppression of the British we are not free.	Britain has "an ancient right" to tax and rule colonies; assumes the need for colonial dependence (e.g., economic and financial factors).
Implications	Continued British Colonial rule; no independent U.S.	Revolutionary War, eventually leading to development of United States of America.	Continued British Colonial Rule; no independent U.S.

Figure 1.1. *Should the colonists support Patrick Henry's ideas? Sample responses.*

make a broad idea. Have students develop a generalization about freedom, based on they've learned so far in the lesson.

2. Explain that in this unit, they will focus on three major generalizations related to the concept of freedom. They are:
   a. Freedom requires sacrifice.
   b. Freedom requires responsibility.
   c. Freedom is threatened by internal and external forces.

   ▪ Consider writing these generalizations on butcher paper or on the board for the duration of the unit. Throughout the unit, other generalizations can be added as students gain more insight into the concept of freedom. Remember that a generalization is a statement that can be applied universally, so these should remain broad.

3. Students can reflect on how the generalizations are supported by Patrick Henry's speech. Some sample responses are shown in Figure 1.2.

Choice-Based Differentiated Products

Students may choose one of the following as independent products to complete (*Note*: Use Rubric 1: Product Rubric in Appendix C to assess student products):

Freedom requires sacrifice.
Henry declares that the only other choice to freedom is death, which is the ultimate sacrifice.
Freedom requires responsibility.
Henry asserts that the colonists must responsibly take action and fight.
Freedom is threatened by internal and external forces.
Freedom is externally threatened by the British authority; freedom is internally threatened by the colonists being deceived that peace is possible without war.

Figure 1.2. Sample student responses to freedom generalizations.

- Write an editorial from the perspective of either a Loyalist or a Patriot in response to Patrick Henry's speech. Provide a positive or negative critique (depending on your point of view) by citing at least three quotes from the speech.
- Examine two pieces of propaganda from either the Patriot or Loyalist perspective. Explain the effect of specific rhetorical techniques used and explain how each piece of propaganda either promotes freedom or denies freedom to a specific group.
- Draw a political cartoon or abstract illustration showing the principles delivered in Patrick Henry's speech. Include a written description to accompany your illustration that describes how it relates to a generalization about freedom.
- Patrick Henry opposed the ratification of the Constitution. Read the excerpt from "Shall Liberty or Empire Be Sought" and conduct a rhetorical analysis to study how Henry develops his argument against the establishment of the American presidency.

Social Studies Content Connections

Refer to the Social Studies Connection Wheel (see Appendix A for information and examples, and Appendix B for a Blank Social Studies Connection Wheel and Social Studies Connections Wheel Guide) to guide students in relating social studies content to the text. The questions below focus on the historical context of the speech. "Social studies factors" refer to any element of the Social Studies Connection Wheel. "Text dependent" means the answer to the question can be gathered by reading the text; "content dependent" means the answer is dependent on social studies content knowledge. Guide students to see how multiple factors interact to cause problems or develop new ideas. The wheel may be referred to visually or students may make connections by writing on a Blank Social Studies

	Effective Rhetoric
0	Provides no response.
1	Response is limited and vague. Response only partially answers the question. A rhetorical element is not mentioned.
2	Response is accurate with one to two rhetorical elements named. Response includes limited or no evidence from text. OR Response includes evidence from text, but does not relate to a rhetorical element.
3	Response is appropriate and accurate describing one to two rhetorical elements to support effective argumentation. Response includes some evidence from the text.
4	Response is insightful and well supported, describing two to three rhetorical elements. Response includes evidence from the text.

Figure 1.3. Scoring guidelines for Lesson 1 formative assessment.

Connections Wheel. The Big Idea Reflection: Primary Sources (Appendix B) can also be used to relate the text to historical content.

- **Text dependent:** According to the speech, what is Patrick Henry's solution to the problem with Britain? Provide an explanation with at least two social studies factors from the Social Studies Connections Wheel in your answer.
- **Content dependent:** What were the economic and political factors that led to the conflict between the colonies and Britain?
- **Content dependent:** What are the long-term implications of the passionate plea "Give me liberty, or give me death"? Explain a cause-effect succession that includes at least three social studies factors from the Social Studies Connection Wheel.

ELA Practice Task

Assign the following task as a performance-based assessment for this lesson: *How does Patrick Henry evoke a sense of urgency for his audience? Explain in a well-developed essay, referring to specific techniques Henry uses to develop and convey his argument.*

Formative Assessment

1. Ask students to respond to the following prompt in a single paragraph: *How effective is Patrick Henry in developing his argument? Support your answer by referring to elements of effective argumentation. Use the Blank Rhetorical Analysis Wheel to organize your thoughts.*
2. Use the scoring guidelines in Figure 1.3 to evaluate students' responses.

Handout 1.1

"Give Me Liberty or Give Me Death" *by Patrick Henry*

Delivered March 23, 1775

MR. PRESIDENT: No man thinks more highly than I do of the patriotism, as well as abilities, of the very worthy gentlemen who have just addressed the House. But different men often see the same subject in different lights; and, therefore, I hope it will not be thought disrespectful to those gentlemen if, entertaining as I do, opinions of a character very opposite to theirs, I shall speak forth my sentiments freely, and without reserve. This is no time for ceremony. The question before the House is one of awful moment to this country. For my own part, I consider it as nothing less than a question of freedom or slavery; and in proportion to the magnitude of the subject ought to be the freedom of the debate. It is only in this way that we can hope to arrive at truth, and fulfill the great responsibility which we hold to God and our country. Should I keep back my opinions at such a time, through fear of giving offence, I should consider myself as guilty of treason towards my country, and of an act of disloyalty toward the majesty of heaven, which I revere above all earthly kings.

Mr. President, it is natural to man to indulge in the illusions of hope. We are apt to shut our eyes against a painful truth, and listen to the song of that siren till she transforms us into beasts. Is this the part of wise men, engaged in a great and arduous struggle for liberty? Are we disposed to be of the number of those who, having eyes, see not, and, having ears, hear not, the things which so nearly concern their temporal salvation? For my part, whatever anguish of spirit it may cost, I am willing to know the whole truth; to know the worst, and to provide for it.

I have but one lamp by which my feet are guided; and that is the lamp of experience. I know of no way of judging of the future but by the past. And judging by the past, I wish to know what there has been in the conduct of the British ministry for the last ten years, to justify those hopes with which gentlemen have been pleased to solace themselves, and the House? Is it that insidious smile with which our petition has been lately received? Trust it not, sir; it will prove a snare to your feet. Suffer not yourselves to be betrayed with a kiss. Ask yourselves how this gracious reception of our petition comports with these war-like preparations which cover our waters and darken our land. Are fleets and armies necessary to a work of love and reconciliation? Have we shown ourselves so unwilling to be reconciled, that force must be called in to win back our love? Let us not deceive ourselves, sir. These are the implements of war and subjugation; the last arguments to which kings resort. I ask, gentlemen, sir, what means this martial array, if its purpose be not to force us to submission? Can gentlemen assign any other possible motive for it? Has Great Britain any enemy, in this quarter of the world, to call for all this accumulation of navies and armies? No, sir, she has none. They are meant for us; they can be meant for no other. They are sent over to bind and rivet upon us those chains which the British ministry have been so long forging. And what have we to oppose to them? Shall we try argument? Sir, we have been

Handout 1.1, Continued

trying that for the last ten years. Have we anything new to offer upon the subject? Nothing. We have held the subject up in every light of which it is capable; but it has been all in vain. Shall we resort to entreaty and humble supplication? What terms shall we find which have not been already exhausted? Let us not, I beseech you, sir, deceive ourselves. Sir, we have done everything that could be done, to avert the storm which is now coming on. We have petitioned; we have remonstrated; we have supplicated; we have prostrated ourselves before the throne, and have implored its interposition to arrest the tyrannical hands of the ministry and Parliament. Our petitions have been slighted; our remonstrances have produced additional violence and insult; our supplications have been disregarded; and we have been spurned, with contempt, from the foot of the throne. In vain, after these things, may we indulge the fond hope of peace and reconciliation. There is no longer any room for hope. If we wish to be free if we mean to preserve inviolate those inestimable privileges for which we have been so long contending if we mean not basely to abandon the noble struggle in which we have been so long engaged, and which we have pledged ourselves never to abandon until the glorious object of our contest shall be obtained, we must fight! I repeat it, sir, we must fight! An appeal to arms and to the God of Hosts is all that is left us!

They tell us, sir, that we are weak; unable to cope with so formidable an adversary. But when shall we be stronger? Will it be the next week, or the next year? Will it be when we are totally disarmed, and when a British guard shall be stationed in every house? Shall we gather strength by irresolution and inaction? Shall we acquire the means of effectual resistance, by lying supinely on our backs, and hugging the delusive phantom of hope, until our enemies shall have bound us hand and foot? Sir, we are not weak if we make a proper use of those means which the God of nature hath placed in our power. Three millions of people, armed in the holy cause of liberty, and in such a country as that which we possess, are invincible by any force which our enemy can send against us. Besides, sir, we shall not fight our battles alone. There is a just God who presides over the destinies of nations; and who will raise up friends to fight our battles for us. The battle, sir, is not to the strong alone; it is to the vigilant, the active, the brave. Besides, sir, we have no election. If we were base enough to desire it, it is now too late to retire from the contest. There is no retreat but in submission and slavery! Our chains are forged! Their clanking may be heard on the plains of Boston! The war is inevitable and let it come! I repeat it, sir, let it come.

It is in vain, sir, to extenuate the matter. Gentlemen may cry, Peace, Peace but there is no peace. The war is actually begun! The next gale that sweeps from the north will bring to our ears the clash of resounding arms! Our brethren are already in the field! Why stand we here idle? What is it that gentlemen wish? What would they have? Is life so dear, or peace so sweet, as to be purchased at the price of chains and slavery? Forbid it, Almighty God! I know not what course others may take; but as for me, give me liberty or give me death!

Handout 1.2
Blank Rhetorical Analysis Wheel

Directions: Draw arrows across elements to show connections.

Text: _____

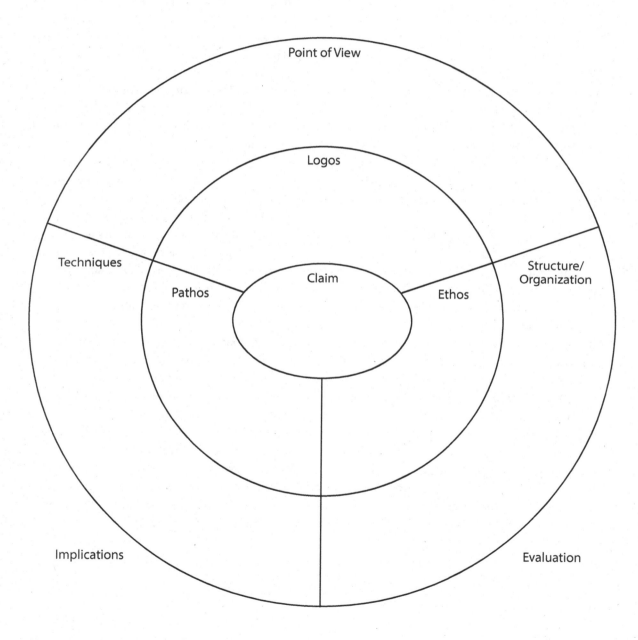

Created by Emily Mofield, Ed.D., & Tamra Stambaugh, Ph.D., 2015.

Name: _____ Date: _____

Handout 1.3
Reasoning About a Situation or Event

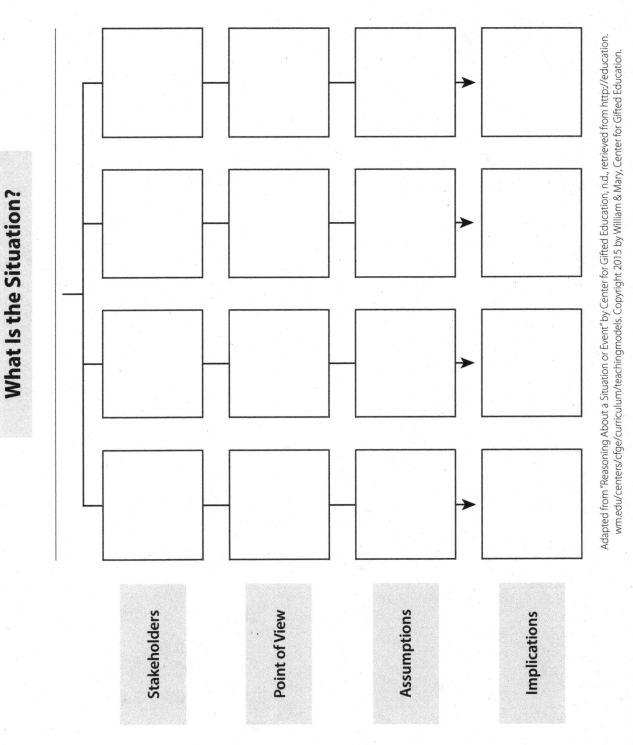

What Is the Situation?

Stakeholders

Point of View

Assumptions

Implications

Lesson

2

"Proclamation Upon British Depredations, Burning of the Capitol"
by James Madison

Goals/Objectives

Content: To analyze and interpret primary source texts, students will be able to:
- explain with evidence how a writer develops and supports a claim,
- respond to interpretations of historical speeches through a variety of contexts,
- compare and contrast various texts and real-world events on themes and generalizations, and
- evaluate rhetorical devices that influence effective argumentation within primary source documents.

Process: To develop thinking, writing, and communication, students will be able to:
- reason through an issue by analyzing points of view, assumptions, and implications;
- use evidence to develop appropriate inferences;
- evaluate use of effective argumentation;
- analyze primary sources (purpose, assumptions, consequences); and
- analyze societal or individual conflicts resulting from the struggle for freedom.

Concept: To understand the theme of freedom and related generalizations, students will be able to:
- support freedom generalizations with evidence from texts;
- apply inductive reasoning to develop generalizations relating to the concepts of freedom, security, individuals, diversity, equality, and democracy;
- describe external and internal threats to personal and national freedom; and
- examine definitions of freedom, means and motives for achieving freedom, and implications for freedom.

DOI: 10.4324/9781003235217-5

Materials

- Student copies of first portion of George W. Bush's 2002 State of the Union Address, available at http://www.washingtonpost.com/wp-srv/onpolitics/transcripts/sou012902.htm
- Handout 2.1: Letter by First Lady Dolley Madison
- Handout 2.2: "Proclamation Upon British Depredations, Burning of the Capitol" by James Madison
- Handout 2.3: Blank Rhetorical Analysis Wheel
- Handout 2.4: Reasoning About a Situation or Event
- Handout 2.5: Concept Organizer
- Rubric 1: Product Rubric (Appendix C)

Introductory Activities

1. Ask: *What times in history has American soil been directly threatened?* Students will likely think of the attacks on Pearl Harbor and September 11, 2001. Allow students to discuss, then show various drawings of the burning of Washington, DC, from 1814. There are many retrievable online through a basic web search. Ask:
   - What do you think is happening in these pictures?
   - What time period do you think this is from?
   - What do you notice about the facial expressions?
   - What do you notice about the background?
   - What questions do you have about these drawings?
   - What event do you think is portrayed?

   Explain that this is the burning of Washington, DC, by the British in 1814 during the War of 1812. Several government buildings were largely destroyed, including the White House and the buildings holding the House, Senate, and Library of Congress.

2. **Engage students in a quick debate.** Ask: *What is terrorism? Would you consider the burning of the Capitol an act of terrorism? Why or why not? How is this similar or different from the attacks of September 11, 2001? Some argue terrorism is a new phenomenon; is it?*

3. Pass out Handout 2.1: Letter by First Lady Dolley Madison. Tell students: *Many historians believe that First Lady Dolley Madison wrote this letter to her sister the day before Washington, DC, was burned. Others believe it was written 20 years after the event. According to evidence in the document, what*

do you think? What personal insight does this tell us about the event? What emotions can we sense? How would you characterize Dolley Madison's tone?

Text-Dependent Questions

Distribute Handout 2.2: "Proclamation Upon British Depredations, Burning of the Capitol" by James Madison. Allow students to read the text individually first. Then, read a paragraph at a time aloud, selecting from the following text-dependent questions to lead discussion.

- In what ways does President Madison build sympathy for the U.S. troops at Washington, DC? Note particular words and phrases used to describe the event, the enemy, and the state of the U.S. troops.
- In the Proclamation, President Madison states, " . . . though for a single day only, they wantonly destroyed the public edifices, having no relation in their structure to operations of war . . . . " What can you infer about the meaning of the word "wanton"? (Sample response: Malevolent, malicious, cruel.)
- According to Madison, how might this event affect more than just people in the United States?
- According to the British commander, what justification is given for the burning of the capital?
- How does Madison refute opposing arguments? Is this enough to convince the audience?
- In paragraph 4, note the word choice Madison uses to describe the enemy's actions. What effect does this have on the audience?
- What does Madison want the "good people" of the United States to do? What does he want the military officers to do? (Sample response: He wants them to unite in defending the nation.)
- Examine the paragraph that begins with "On an occasion . . . " What loaded language does Madison use to evoke emotion in the audience? (Sample response: He uses "proud," "patriotic devotion," "destinies," "glory," "Heaven," "blessed," etc.)
- When Madison says, "None will forget what they owe to themselves, what they owe to their country and the high destinies which await," what exactly do they owe themselves? (Sample response: Defending freedom, independence, and the nation.)
- After reading the entire document, what four key words most closely relate to Madison's message? How do you know?

Rhetorical Analysis

Using Handout 2.3: Blank Rhetorical Analysis Wheel, guide students in understanding how the author develops and supports his claim. Students may take notes on the wheel and draw arrows to illustrate connections between elements. See Appendix A for detailed instructions. Sample questions and responses to lead the analysis include:

- **Context/Purpose:**
  - *What is the historical context?* Madison presented this speech on September 1, 1814, following the attack of the British on the Capitol and Alexandria.
  - *What is Madison's purpose?* His goal is to express disdain regarding Britain's attack and call upon citizens to defend the nation.

- **Claim:**
  - *What is Madison's main claim?* The British caused great devastation; the American people must unite, be vigilant, and be prepared to defend the nation.

- **Point of View/Assumptions:**
  - *What are Madison's assumptions?* Madison assumes that it is not an appropriate retaliation of the British for Americans to attack in Upper Canada.

- **Logos/Technique/Structure:**
  - *How does Madison use reasoning to present his points? What techniques are used and how is his reasoning organized?*
    - **Logos/Reasoning:** He states the problem, discusses the problem's effects, acknowledges Britain's justifications for the attack, provides a rebuttal, appeals to principles of humanity, requests action from the American people, and closes with an appeal to devotion to independence.
    - **Techniques:** He addresses the counterclaim by providing a rebuttal—the British claim they are retaliating from the attacks in Upper Canada, "but no destruction has been committed." He gives facts about the destruction and its effects on the national treasures and inhabitants.
    - **Structure:** This is structured deductively as a "since . . . then" argument. Since the British acted barbarically in their attacks, Madison proclaims that the American people unite and provide adequate defense.

■ **Pathos/Technique/Structure:**

- *How does Madison develop emotional appeals?* He builds sympathy for U.S. troops by saying they are "less numerous," uses loaded language throughout to evoke a sense of anger and disdain ("wanton destruction", "barbaric"), and uses positive loaded words to evoke patriotism and unity ("exhorting all the good of the people . . . ").

■ **Ethos/Technique/Structure:**

- *How does Madison develop credibility and trust?* Madison acknowledges the opposing side—the British claim they made this attack as a retaliation—then he provides a rebuttal and brings credibility by further explaining that the attack was made during a time of negotiating peace.

■ **Implications:**

- *What are the implications/consequences of this document?* This led to a recommitment against the enemy, in the name of defending freedom.

■ **Evaluation:**

- *How effective is the author in supporting his claim?* The proclamation focuses on the devastation caused by the British to incite action from the America people. The focus on the problem (devastation) logically leads to the explanation of the American people uniting in defending themselves.

In-Class Activities to Deepen Learning

1. Have students compare and contrast Madison's speech (Handout 2.1) to George W. Bush's 2002 State of the Union address, which commented on the attacks of September 11, 2001. (*Note:* Consider assigning just the first section until "Our first priority must always be the security of our nation . . . ") Students should examine similarities and differences between Bush's and Madison's approaches and create a Venn diagram or a comparison chart. They should minimally consider ways in which the enemy is described, rhetorical techniques, and approaches to defend freedom. Ask: *What conclusions can you draw regarding their arguments for defending freedom?*

2. Have students complete Handout 2.4: Reasoning About a Situation or Event. Students may be invited to read additional research. Ask: *Was the burning of the Capitol just revenge by British? Consider both British and American points of view* (sample responses are provided in Figure 2.1).

	British	American
Point of View	Yes. This is a retaliation for attacks in Upper Canada.	No. "No destruction has been committed" in reference to Upper Canada.
Assumptions	The Americans have acted aggressively throughout the war. This is rightful retaliation.	The burning of the Capitol was an act of deliberate vandalism during times of negotiating peace. The British destroyed works of art, not relevant to operations of war.
Implications	It is a victory for Britain. The attack intended to make a psychological impact on the enemy (U.S.).	It led to heightened distrust against British and united citizens and military in defense.

Figure 2.1. Was the burning of the Capitol just revenge by the British? Sample responses.

Concept Connections

Guide students to understand how Madison's "Proclamation Upon British Depredations, Burning of the Capitol" exemplifies freedom generalizations by leading them in a discussion using Handout 2.5: Concept Organizer (*Note:* You will use this handout throughout the unit. Use the first column for this lesson). Students should list examples about how the work demonstrates some of the generalizations. Figure 2.2 provides some sample responses. Note that in this lesson, the concept of defense is essential in protecting the nation and democratic freedoms of the Constitution. Ask: *What other statements about freedom can you develop based on the patterns and ideas explored today? Develop this by examining the relationship between freedom and other related concepts such as sacrifice, unity, peace, power, authority, individual, society, and others. Write a statement using a combination of two of these terms.*

Choice-Based Differentiated Products

Students may choose one of the following as independent products to complete (*Note*: Use Rubric 1: Product Rubric in Appendix C to assess student products.):

- Find at least three primary source documents related to the burning of Washington, DC, during August 1814. Using evidence from these documents, write a newspaper article describing the event and how it threatened

41

Freedom requires sacrifice.
Madison asks "good people" to sacrificially unite and give according to the purpose of maintaining freedom/independence.
Freedom requires responsibility.
Madison asks American citizens to give and officers to respond with vigilance in defending freedom.
Freedom is threatened by internal and external forces.
The U.S. and its ideals of freedom were threatened by the external attack from the British.
Examine the relationship between freedom and another concept (e.g., power, conflict, change, order).
Freedom must be defended in times of conflict.

Figure 2.2. Sample student responses to freedom generalizations.

national security and freedom. Cite specific evidence from the primary source documents in your newspaper article.

- Find at least three primary source documents related to the burning of Washington, DC, during August 1814. Develop a skit, monologue, or interview that explains the emotions experienced during the event. Include textual evidence from the primary sources within your responses. Be sure to relate how the experience threatens freedom.

- Was the British burning of the Capitol an act of terrorism? Research the meaning of "terrorism" and examine the context of the War of 1812. Develop an argument using evidence from primary source documents and research to support your point of view. Also, explain how the British action of burning the Capitol is or is not similar to the attacks of September 11, 2001.

ELA Practice Task

Assign the following task as a performance-based assessment for this lesson: *Compare President Madison's "Proclamation Upon British Depredations, Burning of the Capitol" to excerpts from George W. Bush's 2002 State of the Union Address. How do they both present similar messages to citizens of the U.S. in response to attacks? Explain how they use similar approaches in developing their messages, citing sufficient, relevant evidence from the texts.*

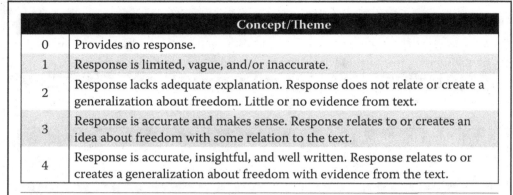

	Concept/Theme
0	Provides no response.
1	Response is limited, vague, and/or inaccurate.
2	Response lacks adequate explanation. Response does not relate or create a generalization about freedom. Little or no evidence from text.
3	Response is accurate and makes sense. Response relates to or creates an idea about freedom with some relation to the text.
4	Response is accurate, insightful, and well written. Response relates to or creates a generalization about freedom with evidence from the text.

Figure 2.3. Scoring guide for Lesson 2 formative assessment.

Social Studies Content Connections

Refer to the Social Studies Connection Wheel (see Appendix A for information and examples, and Appendix B for a Blank Social Studies Connection Wheel and Social Studies Connections Wheel Guide) to guide students in relating social studies content to the text. The questions below focus on the historical context of the speech. The Big Idea Reflection: Primary Sources (Appendix B) can also be used to relate the text to historical content. Ask students the following:

- **Text dependent:** Explain how Madison addressed at least three social studies factors (e.g., economic, cultural, conflict) within the text. Use textual evidence to explain cause-effect relationships between factors.
- **Content dependent:** What are the economic, cultural, and social implications of the British attack on the Capitol?

Formative Assessment

1. Ask students to respond to the following prompt in a single paragraph: *What does Madison's Proclamation reveal about the big idea of freedom? Support your answer with textual evidence.*
2. Use the scoring guidelines in Figure 2.3 to evaluate students' assessments.

Handout 2.1

Letter by First Lady Dolley Madison

Delivered August 23, 1814

My husband left me yesterday morning to join General Winder. He inquired anxiously whether I had courage or firmness to remain in the President's house until his return on the morrow, or succeeding day, and on my assurance that I had no fear but for him, and the success of our army, he left, beseeching me to take care of myself, and of the Cabinet papers, public and private. I have since received two dispatches from him, written with a pencil. The last is alarming, because he desires I should be ready at a moment's warning to enter my carriage, and leave the city; that the enemy seemed stronger than had at first been reported, and it might happen that they would reach the city with the intention of destroying it. I am accordingly ready; I have pressed as many Cabinet papers into trunks as to fill one carriage; our private property must be sacrificed, as it is impossible to procure wagons for its transportation. I am determined not to go myself until I see Mr. Madison safe, so that he can accompany me, as I hear of much hostility towards him. Disaffection stalks around us. My friends and acquaintances are all gone, even Colonel C. with his hundred, who were stationed as a guard in this inclosure. French John (a faithful servant), with his usual activity and resolution, offers to spike the cannon at the gate, and lay a train of powder, which would blow up the British, should they enter the house. To the last proposition I positively object, without being able to make him understand why all advantages in war may not be taken.

Wednesday Morning, twelve o'clock.—Since sunrise I have been turning my spy-glass in every direction, and watching with unwearied anxiety, hoping to discover the approach of my dear husband and his friends; but, alas! I can descry only groups of military, wandering in all directions, as if there was a lack of arms, or of spirit to fight for their own fireside.

Three o'clock.—Will you believe it, my sister? we have had a battle, or skirmish, near Bladensburg, and here I am still, within sound of the cannon! Mr. Madison comes not. May God protect us! Two messengers, covered with dust, come to bid me fly; but here I mean to wait for him . . . At this late hour a wagon has been procured, and I have had it filled with plate and the most valuable portable articles, belonging to the house. Whether it will reach its destination, the "Bank of Maryland," or fall into the hands of British soldiery, events must determine. Our kind friend, Mr. Carroll, has come to hasten my departure, and in a very bad humor with me, because I insist on waiting until the large picture of General Washington is secured, and it requires to be unscrewed from the wall. This process was found too tedious for these perilous moments; I have ordered the frame to be broken, and the canvas taken out. It is done! and the precious portrait placed in the hands of two gentlemen of New York, for safe keeping. And now, dear sister, I must leave this house, or the retreating army will make me a prisoner in it by filling up the road I am directed to take. When I shall again write to you, or where I shall be to-morrow, I cannot tell!

Handout 2.2

"Proclamation upon British Depredations, Burning of the Capitol" *by James Madison*

September 1, 1814

Whereas the enemy by a sudden incursion have succeeded in invading the capital of the nation, defended at the moment by troops less numerous than their own and almost entirely of the militia, during their possession of which, though for a single day only, they wantonly destroyed the public edifices, having no relation in their structure to operations of war nor used at the time for military annoyance, some of these edifices being also costly monuments of taste and of the arts, and others depositories of the public archives, not only precious to the nation as the memorials of its origin and its early transactions, but interesting to all nations as contributions to the general stock of historical instruction and political science; and

Whereas advantage has been taken of the loss of a fort more immediately guarding the neighboring town of Alexandria to place the town within the range of a naval force too long and too much in the habit of abusing its superiority wherever it can be applied to require as the alternative of a general conflagration an undisturbed plunder of private property, which has been executed in a manner peculiarly distressing to the inhabitants, who had inconsiderately cast themselves upon the justice and generosity of the victor; and

Whereas it now appears by a direct communication from the British commander on the American station to be his avowed purpose to employ the force under his direction "in destroying and laying waste such towns and districts upon the coast as may be found assailable," adding to this declaration the insulting pretext that it is in retaliation for a wanton destruction committed by the army of the United States in Upper Canada, when it is notorious that no destruction has been committed, which, notwithstanding the multiplied outrages previously committed by the enemy was not unauthorized, and promptly shown to be so, and that the United States have been as constant in their endeavors to reclaim the enemy from such outrages by the contrast of their own example as they have been ready to terminate on reasonable conditions the war itself; and

Whereas these proceedings and declared purposes, which exhibit a deliberate disregard of the principles of humanity and the rules of civilized warfare, and which must give to the existing war a character of extended devastation and barbarism at the very moment of negotiations for peace, invited by the enemy himself, leave no prospect of safety to anything within the reach of his predatory and incendiary operations but in manful and universal determination to chastise and expel the invader:

Now, therefore, I, James Madison. President of the United States, do issue this my proclamation, exhorting all the good people thereof to unite their hearts and hands in giving effect to the ample means possessed for that purpose. I enjoin it on all officers, civil and military, to exert themselves in executing the duties with which they are respectively charged; and more especially I require the officers commanding the respective military districts to be vigilant and alert in providing for the defense thereof, for the more effectual accomplishment of which they are authorized to call to the defense of exposed and threatened places portions of the militia most convenient thereto, whether they be or be not parts of the quotas detached for the service of the United States under requisitions of the General Government.

On an occasion which appeals so forcibly to the proud feelings and patriotic devotion of the American people none will forget what they owe to themselves, what they owe to their country and the high destinies which await it, what to the glory acquired by their fathers in establishing the independence which is now to be maintained by their sons with the augmented strength and resources with which time and Heaven had blessed them.

In testimony whereof I have hereunto set my hand and caused the seal of the United States to be affixed to these presents.

Done at the city of Washington, the 1st day of September, A.D. 1814, and of the Independence of the United States the thirty-ninth.

JAMES MADISON.
By the President:
JAMES MONROE,
Secretary of State.

Name: _____   Date: _____

Handout 2.3

Blank Rhetorical Analysis Wheel

Directions: Draw arrows across elements to show connections.

Text: _____

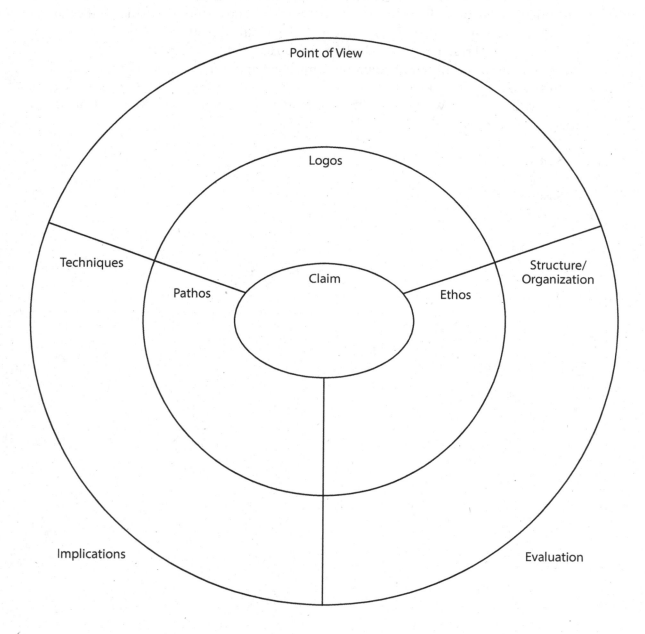

Purpose/Context

Point of View

Logos

Techniques

Claim

Pathos

Ethos

Structure/
Organization

Implications

Evaluation

Created by Emily Mofield, Ed.D., & Tamra Stambaugh, Ph.D., 2015.

Handout 2.4
Reasoning About a Situation or Event

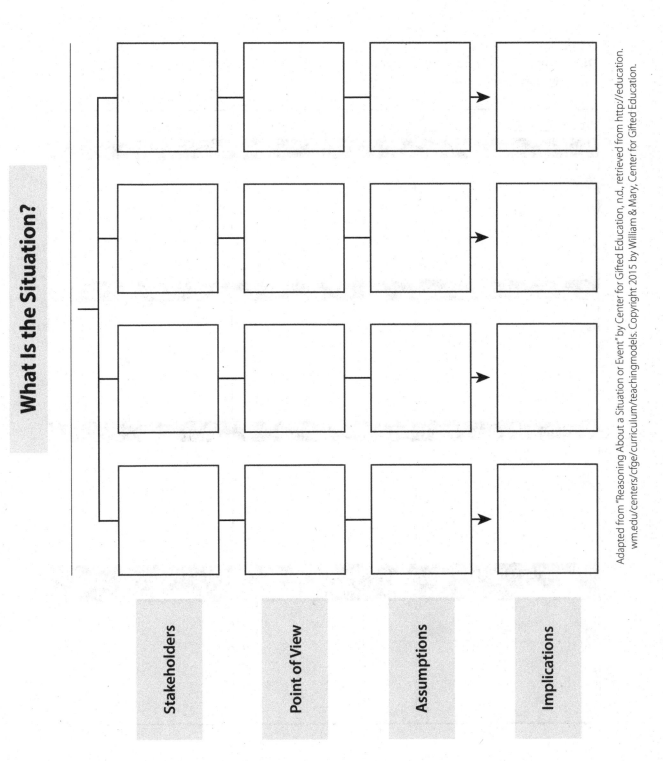

What Is the Situation?

Stakeholders

Point of View

Assumptions

Implications

Name: _____ Date: _____

Handout 2.5
Concept Organizer

Directions: Explain how a selected text exemplifies each freedom generalization. Develop your own generalization.

Text: _____	Text: _____	Text: _____
Freedom requires sacrifice.		
Freedom requires responsibility.		
Freedom is threatened by internal and external forces.		
Examine the relationship between freedom and another concept (e.g., security, power, conflict, change, order, unity, defense, fear, society, individual, etc.).		

Lesson

3

"Speech to Congress on Indian Removal"
by Andrew Jackson

Goals/Objectives

Content: To analyze and interpret primary source texts, students will be able to:
- explain with evidence how a writer develops and supports a claim,
- respond to interpretations of historical speeches through a variety of contexts,
- compare and contrast various texts and real-world events on themes and generalizations, and
- evaluate rhetorical devices that influence effective argumentation within primary source documents.

Process: To develop thinking, writing, and communication, students will be able to:
- reason through an issue by analyzing points of view, assumptions, and implications;
- use evidence to develop appropriate inferences;
- evaluate use of effective argumentation;
- analyze primary sources (purpose, assumptions, consequences); and
- analyze societal or individual conflicts resulting from the struggle for freedom.

Concept: To understand the theme of freedom and related generalizations, students will be able to:
- support freedom generalizations with evidence from texts;
- apply inductive reasoning to develop generalizations relating to the concepts of freedom, security, individuals, diversity, equality, and democracy;
- describe external and internal threats to personal and national freedom; and
- examine definitions of freedom, means and motives for achieving freedom, and implications for freedom.

 DOI: 10.4324/9781003235217-6

Materials

- Student copies of letters by Chief John Ross (*Note*: Many letters can be retrieved online through a basic Google search. We recommend "Our Hearts are Sickened," available at http://historymatters.gmu.edu/d/6598.)
- Handout 3.1: "Speech to Congress on Indian Removal" by Andrew Jackson
- Handout 3.2: Blank Rhetorical Analysis Wheel
- Handout 3.3: Reasoning about a Situation or Event
- Rubric 1: Product Rubric (Appendix C)

Note: As you teach this lesson, guide students to understand the complexity of the cultural context regarding Andrew Jackson's Indian Removal Act. Although Jackson's prejudices are displayed throughout his speech, explain that he had also adopted an Indian child, Lincoya, who lived with him at The Hermitage. This could potentially be an area for additional research for students. Economic factors such as the Georgia gold rush also influenced Indian removal, because gold was on Cherokee land. This led to tensions between White settlers and the Cherokee. Although President Jackson's perspectives and assumptions are extremely biased, they must be understood within the historical context.

Introductory Activities

1. Start the lesson by telling a small group of students (who seem to enjoy their seats) that they have to move. Tell them they must sit on the floor (or somewhere that does not seem fair) for the entire lesson. Also ask them to give up some "property," such as a cell phone, purse, paper, shoe, etc. Ask: *Is it justifiable to take away your property? Is it ever justifiable? What assumptions are made for me to take it away from you?* Explain that students will have an opportunity to explore multiple perspectives toward the Cherokee Nation, particularly on the topic of the Indian Removal Act.
2. You may wish to show a brief video clip about Indian removal or provide some basic information about the Trail of Tears. There are several available online through a basic Google search.

Text-Dependent Questions

Distribute Handout 3.1: "Speech to Congress on Indian Removal" by Andrew Jackson. Allow students to read the text individually first. Then, read a paragraph at a time aloud, selecting from the following text-dependent questions to lead discussion.

- In the first paragraph, what approach does Jackson use to persuade his audience that the removal of "Indians" is a positive event? (Sample response: He uses positive connotations, loaded language.)
- Jackson claims that the tribes moving will experience an "obvious advantage." Is Jackson clear in articulating what the obvious advantage is?
- How many positive consequences does Jackson list for the speedy removal of Indians in paragraph 2? Which ones would be characterized as advantages for the United States? Which ones would be characterized as advantages for the Indians (according to Jackson)? Which "advantages" do you think the American Indians would disagree with? (*Note*: Make sure students understand the term "pecuniary.")
- What statements might be easy for the audience to accept? Which statements might be harder for the audience to accept?
- Jackson states, "What good man would prefer a country covered with forests . . . " Who is the "good man"? What words does Jackson use to describe the American Indians?
- What assumptions are present within the rhetorical question in paragraph 3?
- In what ways does Jackson attempt to address the American Indians' point of view? What arguments from the American Indians' perspective are not included within this document? (Sample response: He attempts to address their point of view with "doubtless, it will be painful to leave the graves of their fathers . . . ")
- What assumptions does Jackson make in the document concerning "our own people"?
- What does Jackson imply will happen to the American Indians if the Indian Removal Act does not happen?
- What does this text reveal about America's journey toward freedom?

Rhetorical Analysis

Using Handout 3.2: Blank Rhetorical Analysis Wheel, guide students in understanding how the author uses effective argumentation techniques. Depending on student readiness, consider asking students to complete the analysis in small groups. Students may take notes on the wheel and draw arrows to illustrate connections between elements. Sample questions and responses to lead the analysis include:

- **Context/Purpose:**
  - *What is the historical context?* Andrew Jackson presented this speech to Congress on December 6, 1830.
  - *What is Jackson's purpose?* His goal is to present a rationale and benefits of the government's plan for Indian removal.

- **Claim:**
  - *What is Jackson's main claim?* It is justifiable and benevolent to remove Indians to a new settlement.

- Point of View/Assumptions:
  - *What are Jackson's assumptions?* Jackson assumes that Indians are not civilized or interesting. He refers to the Indians as savages, implying superiority over them.

- **Logos/Technique/Structure:**
  - *How does Jackson present his points? What techniques are used and how are his points organized?*
    - **Logos/Reasoning:** He introduces the policy, describes consequences of the policy, explains that it a continuation of policies, and concludes with the main thesis.
    - **Techniques:** He provides stark contrast between "good man living in a country covered with forests and ranged by a few thousand savages" versus "an extensive Republic studded with cities, towns, and prosperous farms." He uses analogy to compare Indian removal and settlement to White forefathers who left their land to resettle for better lives. He uses several rhetorical questions to build his argument that the policy of the government is benevolent (especially at the end).
    - **Structure:** Point by point. He lists the advantages of Indian removal.

- **Pathos/Technique/Structure:**
  - *How does Jackson develop emotional appeals?* He builds superior pride among the audience by using loaded language ("pleasure to announce, happy consummation, obvious advantages, liberal and generous."). He references how the Indians evoke a sense of superiority ("savages" in contrast to being "interesting," "civilized," and "Christian").

- **Ethos/Technique/Structure:**
  - *How does Jackson develop credibility and trust?* At the beginning Jackson explains that two tribes have already agreed to the policy; he acknowledges the opposing side while referencing historical precedent ("doubtless it will be painful to leave the graves of their fathers"). His extreme bias lessens ethos appeals.

- **Implications:**
  - *What are the implications of this document?* The implications include Indian removal, the Trail of Tears, and the establishment of White settlements.

- Evaluation:
  - *How effective is the author in supporting his claim?* Jackson presents many logical arguments for Indian removal; however, his bias and point of view lessen his ethos appeals. Although his argument is logical, it is not necessarily considered an ethical argument.

In-Class Activities to Deepen Learning

1. Ask students to read a document from a Cherokee perspective. Several documents, speeches, and letters are available online from Cherokee Chief John Ross (we've listed our recommendation under the Materials section of this lesson). Ask: *From the perspective of a Cherokee, how would you respond to some of Jackson's reasoning?* Students may answer through discussion or writing.
2. Guide students through Handout 3.3: Reasoning About a Situation or Event on the following issue: Should Congress agree to Jackson's proposal on Indian removal?

Note on historical background: The Indian Removal Act did pass in the House and Senate. The Cherokee Nation declared themselves not to be under the control of the U.S., but of their own sovereign nation. Thus, the U.S. government could not directly move them without mutual consent. In 1835, a small group of Cherokees did agree to be moved west of the Mississippi (without the consensus of the majority of the Cherokee). In 1838, U.S. troops marched them along the "Trail of Tears" to Indian Territory west of the Mississippi. More information can be found at http://www.pbs.org/wgbh/aia/part4/4p2959.html.

Concept Connections

1. If possible, display the preamble to the U.S. Constitution and the first sentence of the Declaration of Independence, and discuss with the class the generalizations of freedom that are embodied in both documents.
2. Ask: *In the texts we read today, which ones exemplified ideas of freedom? Do any promote the ideals of America as outlined by our Founding Fathers? How does Andrew Jackson's address refute or support our freedom generalizations?*

Students may record their reflections on Handout 2.5, continuing their notes from Lesson 2 (sample responses are provided in Figure 3.1).

Choice-Based Differentiated Products

Students may choose one of the following as independent products to complete (*Note*: Use Rubric 1: Product Rubric in Appendix C to assess student products):

- Research more about the Trail of Tears. Obtain at least one primary source text from this event. Write a first-person narrative account using your own imagination and information from the primary source text. Allude to how ideals of freedom are not afforded to "all."
- What other ideas could the U.S. government and Cherokee Nation have developed that would have been better than the Indian Removal Act? Develop an action plan describing who, what, when, where, and how life, liberty, and the pursuit of happiness could be for "all," including the Cherokee Nation in 1830.
- Read other primary sources by Cherokee Chief John Ross. Research his background and present a short presentation on his life and influence to the class. Include specific ways in which he hoped to secure freedoms for the Cherokee Nation.
- Read a primary source document related to the Cherokee point of view on the Indian Removal Act. Write a poem from the perspective of a Cherokee as it relates to the idea of Indian removal. Include an idea about freedom within your poem and include an illustration or symbol.

ELA Practice Task

Assign the following task as a performance-based assessment for this lesson: *In a well-developed essay, explain how President Jackson's point of view influenced the development of his central idea in his speech to Congress about Indian removal. Consider how Jackson's assumptions and tone relate to his point of view. Cite evidence from the text to support your response.*

Social Studies Content Connections

Refer to the Social Studies Connection Wheel (see Appendix A for information and examples, and Appendix B for a Blank Social Studies Connection Wheel and Social Studies Connections Wheel Guide) to guide students in relating social studies content to the text. The questions below focus on the historical context of the speech. The Big Idea Reflection: Primary Sources (Appendix B) can also be used to relate the text to historical content. Ask students the following:

Freedom requires sacrifice.
Jackson denies freedom to the American Indians to live in their homeland. In order for the White citizens to have freedom to live on this land, the American Indians had to be moved. This was a major sacrifice.
Freedom requires responsibility.
Students may say Jackson's document disregards this generalization—the U.S. does not consider responsible ways to allow the American Indians to stay on their land.
Freedom is threatened by internal and external forces.
Freedom of the Cherokee to live peacefully in their homeland was threatened by the U.S. government. Jackson would argue freedom for U.S. citizens is threatened by the American Indians' presence.
Examine the relationship between freedom and another concept (e.g., power, conflict, change, order).
When unity is not achieved between two groups, freedom is unequally divided, resulting in oppression of one group.

Figure 3.1. Sample student responses to freedom generalizations.

- **Content dependent:** How did geography and economics interact to influence the U.S government to pass the Indian Removal Act (e.g., discovery of gold in Georgia)?
- **Text dependent:** Jackson establishes several reasons for Indian removal. Explain how these reasons relate to at least three social studies factors from the Social Studies Connections Wheel.
- **Content dependent:** What were the social, cultural, and economic implications of Indian removal for American Indians? For White settlers? How do these three implications relate to each other?

Formative Assessment

1. Ask students to respond to the following prompt in a single paragraph: *What is Andrew Jackson's main claim in "Speech to Congress on Indian Removal" and how is it supported? Provide textual evidence.*
2. Use the scoring guidelines in Figure 3.2 to evaluate students' assessments.

	Claims and Evidence
0	Provides no response.
1	Response is limited, vague, and/or inaccurate. Only the claim is mentioned with little support.
2	Response lacks adequate explanation. Some parts of the response are correct, but the response only vaguely addresses the author's claim and evidence. Response lacks support.
3	Response is accurate and makes sense. Response includes one to two examples of support for the claim.
4	Response is accurate, insightful, and well written. Response includes two to three examples of support for the claim with textual evidence.

Figure 3.2. Scoring guidelines for Lesson 3 formative assessment.

Handout 3.1

"Speech to Congress on Indian Removal" *by Andrew Jackson*

Delivered December 6, 1830

It gives me pleasure to announce to Congress that the benevolent policy of the Government, steadily pursued for nearly thirty years, in relation to the removal of the Indians beyond the white settlements is approaching to a happy consummation. Two important tribes have accepted the provision made for their removal at the last session of Congress, and it is believed that their example will induce the remaining tribes also to seek the same obvious advantages.

The consequences of a speedy removal will be important to the United States, to individual States, and to the Indians themselves. The pecuniary advantages which it promises to the Government are the least of its recommendations. It puts an end to all possible danger of collision between the authorities of the General and State Governments on account of the Indians. It will place a dense and civilized population in large tracts of country now occupied by a few savage hunters. By opening the whole territory between Tennessee on the north and Louisiana on the south to the settlement of the whites it will incalculably strengthen the southwestern frontier and render the adjacent States strong enough to repel future invasions without remote aid. It will relieve the whole State of Mississippi and the western part of Alabama of Indian occupancy, and enable those States to advance rapidly in population, wealth, and power. It will separate the Indians from immediate contact with settlements of whites; free them from the power of the States; enable them to pursue happiness in their own way and under their own rude institutions; will retard the progress of decay, which is lessening their numbers, and perhaps cause them gradually, under the protection of the Government and through the influence of good counsels, to cast off their savage habits and become an interesting, civilized, and Christian community.

What good man would prefer a country covered with forests and ranged by a few thousand savages to our extensive Republic, studded with cities, towns, and prosperous farms embellished with all the improvements which art can devise or industry execute, occupied by more than 12,000,000 happy people, and filled with all the blessings of liberty, civilization and religion?

The present policy of the Government is but a continuation of the same progressive change by a milder process. The tribes which occupied the countries now constituting the Eastern States were annihilated or have melted away to make room for the whites. The waves of population and civilization are rolling to the westward, and we now propose to acquire the countries occupied by the red men of the South and West by a fair exchange, and, at the expense of the United States, to send them to land where their existence may be prolonged and perhaps made perpetual. Doubtless it will be painful to leave the graves of their fathers; but what do they more than our ancestors did or than our children are now doing? To better their condition in an unknown land our forefathers left all that was dear in earthly objects. Our children by thousands yearly leave the land of their birth to seek new homes in distant regions. Does Humanity weep at these painful separations from everything, animate and inanimate, with which the young heart has become entwined? Far from it. It is rather a source of joy that our country affords scope where our young population may range unconstrained in body or in mind, developing the power and facilities of man in their highest perfection. These remove hundreds and almost thousands of miles at their own expense, purchase the lands they occupy, and support themselves at their new homes from the moment of their arrival. Can it be cruel in this Government when, by events which it cannot control, the Indian is made discontented in his ancient home to purchase his lands, to give him a new and extensive territory, to pay the expense of his removal, and support him a year in his new abode? How many thousands of our own people would gladly embrace the opportunity of removing to the West on such conditions! If the offers made to the Indians were extended to them, they would be hailed with gratitude and joy.

And is it supposed that the wandering savage has a stronger attachment to his home than the settled, civilized Christian? Is it more afflicting to him to leave the graves of his fathers than it is to our brothers and children? Rightly considered, the policy of the General Government toward the red man is not only liberal, but generous. He is unwilling to submit to the laws of the States and mingle with their population. To save him from this alternative, or perhaps utter annihilation, the General Government kindly offers him a new home, and proposes to pay the whole expense of his removal and settlement.

Name: _____ Date: _____

Handout 3.2
Blank Rhetorical Analysis Wheel

Directions: Draw arrows across elements to show connections.

Text: _____

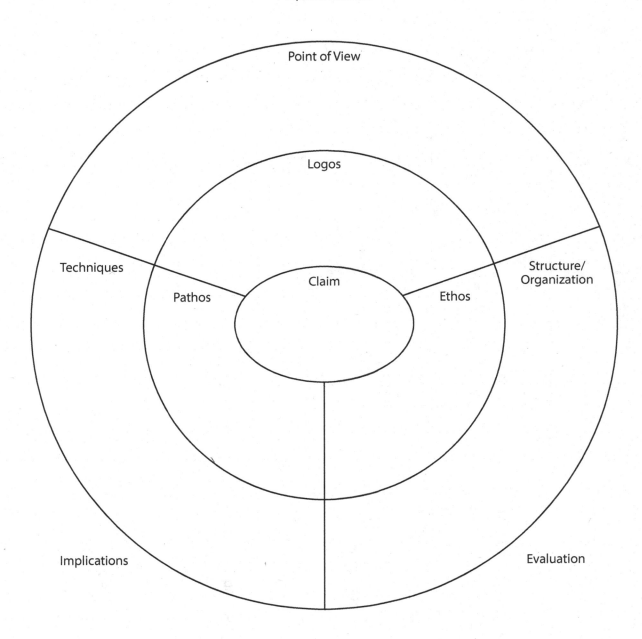

Created by Emily Mofield, Ed.D., & Tamra Stambaugh, Ph.D., 2015.

Finding Freedom © Taylor & Francis

Handout 3.3
Reasoning About a Situation or Event

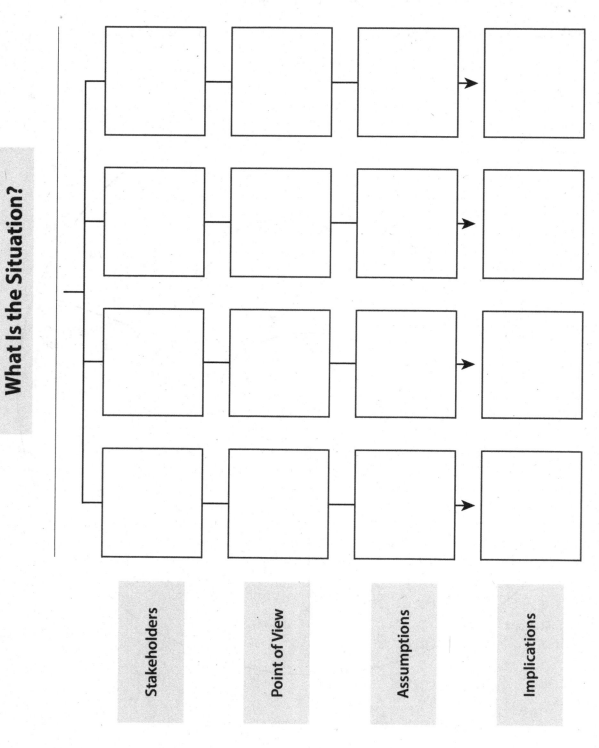

What Is the Situation?

Stakeholders

Point of View

Assumptions

Implications

Adapted from "Reasoning About a Situation or Event" by Center for Gifted Education, n.d., retrieved from http://education.wm.edu/centers/cfge/curriculum/teachingmodels. Copyright 2015 by William & Mary, Center for Gifted Education.

Lesson

4

"The Hypocrisy of the Nation Must Be Exposed"
by Frederick Douglass

Goals/Objectives

Content: To analyze and interpret primary source texts, students will be able to:

- explain with evidence how a writer develops and supports a claim,
- respond to interpretations of historical speeches through a variety of contexts,
- compare and contrast various texts and real-world events on themes and generalizations, and
- evaluate rhetorical devices that influence effective argumentation within primary source documents.

Process: To develop thinking, writing, and communication, students will be able to:

- use evidence to develop appropriate inferences;
- evaluate use of effective argumentation;
- analyze primary sources (purpose, assumptions, consequences); and
- analyze societal or individual conflicts resulting from the struggle for freedom.

Concept: To understand the theme of freedom and related generalizations, students will be able to:

- support freedom generalizations with evidence from texts;
- apply inductive reasoning to develop generalizations relating to the concepts of freedom, security, individuals, diversity, equality, and democracy;
- describe external and internal threats to personal and national freedom; and
- examine definitions of freedom, means and motives for achieving freedom, and implications for freedom.

DOI: 10.4324/9781003235217-7

Materials

- Student copies of an excerpt from William John Grayson's *The Hireling and the Slave* (*Note*: This text is optional and the teacher can choose any other proslavery historical text if preferred.)
- Handout 4.1: "The Hypocrisy of the Nation Must Be Exposed" by Frederick Douglass
- Handout 4.2: Blank Rhetorical Analysis Wheel
- Handout 4.3: Freedom Chart
- Rubric 1: Product Rubric (Appendix C)

Introductory Activities

1. Explain that students will be reading a text by Frederick Douglass. Provide brief background information about him:
   - He was born into slavery in 1817.
   - He taught himself how to read and write and escaped slavery in 1838.
   - He is one of the most famous abolitionists in American history.

2. Explain to students that even though today it seems obvious that slavery is absolutely wrong, the culture of the 1850s, especially in the Southern states, was quite different. Ask students to examine a document that argued for slavery, such as excerpts from William John Grayson's *The Hireling and the Slave*. Explain that the arguments in the document are extremely biased, as they were arguments used to support the atrocity of slavery. Contrary to the excerpt, if one reads Frederick Douglass's autobiography, *Narrative of the Life of Frederick Douglass*, one will see a clear picture of how some slaves were treated and abused.

3. After reading the excerpt, ask: *What is your reaction to these pro-slavery arguments? How would you argue against slavery?* After discussion, note a quote from Abraham Lincoln (1865):

   I have always thought that all men should be free; but if any should be slaves it should be first those who desire it for themselves, and secondly those who desire it for others. When I hear anyone arguing for slavery, I feel a strong impulse to see it tried on him personally. (para. 2)

Text-Dependent Questions

Distribute Handout 4.1: "The Hypocrisy of a Nation Must Be Exposed" by Fredrick Douglass. Allow students to read the text individually first. Then, read a paragraph at a time aloud, selecting from the following text-dependent questions to lead discussion.

- How would you describe Douglass's tone in his introduction?
- How does parallelism help develop his reasoning in the second paragraph? (Sample response: Douglass presents several contrasts between slaves and the free: "Liberty is enjoyed by your fathers, not me . . .," ". . . sunlight brought you life, but brought me death . . . ")
- What is meant by "America is false to the past, false to the present, and solemnly binds herself to be false to the future?"
- According to Douglass, what is treason? What is the denotation and connotation of the word "treason"? Why does he choose this particular word to make his point?
- What is Douglass's main claim in the subsequent paragraphs and how does he support this argument? (Sample response: Douglass claims slaves are men—they are punished by law, the animals can tell no difference between a slave and a free man.)
- How does he incorporate deductive logic of syllogisms to develop his argument? (Sample response: Slaves are men, men are entitled to liberty, so slaves are entitled to liberty.)
- What effect does the repetition of rhetorical questions have on his message? How would the effect be different if these were statements? (Sample response: Rhetorical questions elicit personal reflection.)
- What literary pattern is Douglass establishing in the paragraph which begins as "At a time like this, scorching irony . . . ?" How does he use parallelism and repetition in this paragraph and what effect does it have? (Sample response: There is continued use of parallelism and contrasts, emphasis on related ideas, moving toward more intense emotions.)
- After reading the last two paragraphs, what do you consider to be Douglass's most significant accusation on America?
- If you had to divide the speech into three parts, what would they be and how would you label them?
- What statement from the speech is most powerful? Why?

Rhetorical Analysis

Using Handout 4.2: Blank Rhetorical Analysis Wheel, guide students in analyzing how the author uses effective argumentation techniques. Students may take notes on the wheel and draw arrows to illustrate connections between elements. Sample question and responses to lead analysis include:

- **Context/Purpose:**
  - *What is the historical context?* Fredrick Douglass presented this speech on July 4, 1852, in Rochester, NY, where he was invited to speak to commemorate Independence Day. Rochester was considered his adopted hometown, where he lived and edited an abolitionist newspaper. Douglass also delivered another famous speech, "What to the Slave Is the Fourth of July," on July 5, 1852, that contains similar ideas.
  - *What is Douglass's purpose?* His goal is to expose the hypocrisy of America as it celebrates liberty that is not given to all men.

- **Claim:**
  - *What is Douglass's main claim?* The hypocrisy of America must be exposed: Slaves are men and men should be free.

- **Point of View/Assumptions:**
  - *What is Douglass's point of view and what are his assumptions?* Douglass speaks from the perspective of a slave, but also a man. He assumes that all men should be free.

- **Logos/Technique/Structure:**
  - *How does Douglass use reasoning to present his main points? How are they developed and how are they organized?*
    - **Logos/Reasoning:** He presents questions, exposes that liberty is not shared by all, and explains that slavery is wrong and unjust, slaves are men, and the Fourth of July reveals the shameless hypocrisy of America.
    - **Techniques:** He uses syllogism and deductive reasoning to develop his argument that slaves are men (slaves are men, men are free, so slaves should be free), uses parallelism in the second paragraph to develop disparity between slaves and the free, and uses repetition of rhetorical questions to build intensity and evoke reflection in his points.
    - **Structure:** Deductive. He presents his purpose and topic at the beginning of the speech and supports it throughout, point by point.

- **Pathos/Technique/Structure:**
  - *How does Douglass develop emotional appeals?* He evokes sympathy for the slave and himself (he is not included in the celebrations of the Fourth of July), further evokes sympathy through metaphor and contrast ("the

sunlight that brought life and healing to you has brought stripes and death to me"), builds a sense of shame on America through loaded language and negative connotations (bombast, fraud, deception), and elicits a sense of urgency through tone, especially toward the end.

- **Ethos/Technique/Structure:**
  - *How does Douglass develop credibility and trust?* He himself was a slave, adding credibility to his perspectives; he refers to the Constitution and Bible as sources that show the "great sin" of slavery.

- **Implications:**
  - *What are the implications/consequences of this document?* This was part of the abolitionist movement, during which ideas about the injustice of slavery spread.

- **Evaluation:**
  - *How effective is the author in supporting his claim?* The speech passionately presents an argument that America is a nation of hypocrisy. Douglass uses several techniques to appeal to reasoning (logos). His use of syllogisms is especially important. His ethos appeals are strong with support from the Constitution and Bible. He effectively presents pathos appeals without emotional manipulation.

In-Class Activity to Deepen Learning

Ask students to compare and contrast Patrick Henry's perspective (Lesson 1) for pursuing freedom to Frederick Douglass's. Consider threats to freedom and ways to achieve freedom. Also consider similarities in their urgent tone. Develop a Venn diagram or comparison chart.

Concept Connections

1. Discuss connections to freedom by asking the following questions:
   - According to Douglass, how is the character of America a threat to freedom?
   - What paradoxes does Douglass reveal about freedom?
   - The students can add their reflections to Handout 2.5: Concept Organizer. Figure 4.1 contains some sample student responses.

2. Have students complete Handout 4.3: Freedom Chart to further examine concept connections. In later lessons, students may continue to add to this chart.

Freedom requires sacrifice.
Douglass argues freedom for the slaves should not require these arguments presented; freedom belongs to slaves because they are "men," therefore freedom should not require additional sacrifice for them. This is a self-evident principle.
Freedom requires responsibility.
Douglass asserts that it is treason for him to forget the plight of slavery—he takes responsibility in exposing the hypocrisy of America in order to promote liberty for slaves.
Freedom is threatened by internal and external forces.
Freedom is threatened by the hypocrisy of America's character.
Examine the relationship between freedom and another concept (e.g., power, conflict, change, order).
Consider the paradox: Slavery exists within a nation that claims to be devoted to freedom.

Figure 4.1. Sample student responses.

Choice-Based Differentiated Products

Students may choose one of the following as independent products to complete (*Note*: Use Rubric 1: Product Rubric in Appendix C to assess student products.):

- Find a primary source document that uses scientific or religious arguments to promote Southern slavery. Conduct a rhetorical analysis using The Rhetorical Analysis Wheel. Then, write an editorial (from the perspective of someone in the 1800s) in response to reading the sources, critiquing the argument presented. Consider using evidence or quotes from Douglass's text in your editorial.
- Read a chapter from Frederick Douglass's autobiography, *Narrative of the Life of Frederick Douglass* (the full text is widely accessible online). Write a reflection as a response to your reading. Answer the following questions in your reflection: What challenges did Douglass face and how did he persevere through them? What does the text reveal about his character and personality? How were his thoughts, behaviors, and actions influenced by individuals mentioned in the text? How does this information shed insight into his speech "The Hypocrisy of a Nation Must Be Exposed"?
- Write a dialogue between Frederick Douglass and Patrick Henry discussing their common desire for freedom. Include at least three quotes from each individual (from their speeches or other sources). Include questions they may ask of each other and their hopes for the future of the United States.

ELA Practice Task

Assign the following task as a performance-based assessment for this lesson: *In a multiparagraph essay, compare and contrast Frederick Douglass's "The Hypocrisy of a Nation Must Be Exposed," presented July 4, 1852, to "What to the Slave Is the Fourth of July?," presented July 5, 1852. Compare and contrast his techniques in developing his argument in both speeches. Include relevant and sufficient evidence to support your analysis. (Note: The latter speech is accessible online.)*

Social Studies Content Connections

Refer to the Social Studies Connection Wheel (see Appendix A for information and examples, and Appendix B for a Blank Social Studies Connection Wheel and Social Studies Connections Wheel Guide) to guide students in relating social studies content to the text. The questions below focus on the historical context of the speech. The Big Idea Reflection: Primary Sources (Appendix B) can also be used to relate the text to historical content.

- **Content dependent:** How did economics, culture, and geography connect to the issue of slavery? What patterns do you notice among these? Write three generalizations.
- **Text dependent:** How does Douglass connect world context to the development of his message? Why is this important?
- **Text dependent:** What action does Frederick Douglass's message imply? In your response, address at least three social studies factors from the Social Studies Connections Wheel.

Formative Assessment

1. Ask students to respond to the following prompt in a single paragraph: *How effective is Frederick Douglass in developing his argument? Support your answer by referring to elements of effective argumentation.*
2. Use the scoring guidelines in Figure 4.2 to evaluate students' assessments.

	Effective Rhetoric
0	Provides no response.
1	Response is limited and vague. Response only partially answers the question. A rhetorical element is not mentioned.
2	Response is accurate with one to two rhetorical elements named. Response includes limited or no evidence from text. OR Response includes evidence from text, but does not relate to a rhetorical element.
3	Response is appropriate and accurate, describing one to two rhetorical elements to support effective argumentation. Response includes some evidence from the text.
4	Response is insightful and well supported, describing two to three rhetorical elements. Response includes evidence from the text.

Figure 4.2. Scoring guidelines for Lesson 4 formative assessment.

Handout 4.1

Excerpts From "The Hypocrisy of the Nation Must Be Exposed" *by Frederick Douglass*

Delivered July 4, 1852

Fellow citizens, pardon me, and allow me to ask, why am I called upon to speak here today? What have I or those I represent to do with your national independence? Are the great principles of political freedom and of natural justice, embodied in that Declaration of Independence, extended to us? And am I, therefore, called upon to bring our humble offering to the national altar, and to confess the benefits, and express devout gratitude for the blessings resulting from your independence to us? . . .

. . . I am not included within the pale of this glorious anniversary! Your high independence only reveals the immeasurable distance between us. The blessings in which you this day rejoice are not enjoyed in common. The rich inheritance of justice, liberty, prosperity, and independence bequeathed by your fathers is shared by you, not by me. The sunlight that brought life and healing to you has brought stripes and death to me. This Fourth of July is yours, not mine. You may rejoice, I must mourn. To drag a man in fetters into the grand illuminated temple of liberty, and call upon him to join you in joyous anthems, were inhuman mockery and sacrilegious irony. Do you mean, citizens, to mock me, by asking me to speak today? If so, there is a parallel to your conduct. And let me warn you, that it is dangerous to copy the example of a nation (Babylon) whose crimes, towering up to heaven, were thrown down by the breath of the Almighty, burying that nation in irrecoverable ruin.

Fellow citizens, above your national, tumultuous joy, I hear the mournful wail of millions, whose chains, heavy and grievous yesterday, are today rendered more intolerable by the jubilant shouts that reach them. If I do forget, if I do not remember those bleeding children of sorrow this day, "may my right hand forget her cunning, and may my tongue cleave to the roof of my mouth!"

To forget them, to pass lightly over their wrongs and to chime in with the popular theme would be treason most scandalous and shocking, and would make me a reproach before God and the world.

My subject, then, fellow citizens, is "American Slavery." I shall see this day and its popular characteristics from the slave's point of view. Standing here, identified with the American bondman, making his wrongs mine, I do not hesitate to declare, with all my soul, that the character and conduct of this nation never looked blacker to me than on this Fourth of July.

Whether we turn to the declarations of the past, or to the professions of the present, the conduct of the nation seems equally hideous and revolting. America is false to the past, false to the present, and solemnly binds herself to be false to the future. Standing with God and the crushed and bleeding slave on this occasion, I will, in the name of humanity, which is outraged, in the name of liberty, which is fettered, in the name of the Constitution and the Bible, which are disregarded and trampled upon, dare to call in question and to denounce, with all the emphasis I can command, everything that serves to perpetuate slavery—the great sin and shame of America! "I will not equivocate—I will not excuse." I will use the severest language I can command, and yet not one word shall escape me that any man, whose judgment is not blinded by prejudice, or who is not at heart a slave-holder, shall not confess to be right and just.

. . . Must I undertake to prove that the slave is a man? That point is conceded already. Nobody doubts it. The slave-holders themselves acknowledge it in the enactment of laws for their government. They acknowledge it when they punish disobedience on the part of the slave. There are seventy-two crimes in the State of Virginia, which, if committed by a black man (no matter how ignorant he be), subject him to the punishment of death; while only two of these same crimes will subject a white man to like punishment.

What is this but the acknowledgment that the slave is a moral, intellectual, and responsible being? The manhood of the slave is conceded. It is admitted in the fact that Southern statute books are covered with enactments, forbidding, under severe fines and penalties, the teaching of the slave to read and write. When you can point to any such laws in reference to the beasts of the field, then I may consent to argue the manhood of the slave. When the dogs in your streets, when the fowls of the air, when the cattle on your hills, when the fish of the sea, and the reptiles that crawl, shall be unable to distinguish the slave from a brute, then I will argue with you that the slave is a man!

For the present it is enough to affirm the equal manhood of the Negro race. Is it not astonishing that, while we are plowing, planting, and reaping, using all kinds of mechanical tools, erecting houses, constructing bridges, building ships, working in metals of brass, iron, copper, silver, and gold; that while we are reading, writing, and ciphering, acting as clerks, merchants, and secretaries, having among us lawyers, doctors, ministers, poets, authors, editors, orators, and teachers; that we are engaged in all the enterprises common to other men—digging gold in California, capturing the whale in the Pacific, feeding sheep and cattle on the hillside, living, moving, acting, thinking, planning, living in families as husbands, wives, and children, and above all, confessing and worshipping the Christian God, and looking hopefully for life and immortality beyond the grave—we are called upon to prove that we are men?

Would you have me argue that man is entitled to liberty? That he is the rightful owner of his own body? You have already declared it. Must I argue the wrongfulness of slavery? . . .

What! Am I to argue that it is wrong to make men brutes, to rob them of their liberty, to work them without wages, to keep them ignorant of their relations to their fellow men, to beat them with sticks, to flay their flesh with the lash, to load their limbs with irons, to hunt them with dogs, to sell them at auction, to sunder their families, to knock out their teeth, to burn their flesh, to starve them into obedience and submission to their masters? Must I argue that a system thus marked with blood and stained with pollution is wrong? No—I will not. I have better employment for my time and strength than such arguments would imply.

What, then, remains to be argued? Is it that slavery is not divine; that God did not establish it; that our doctors of divinity are mistaken? There is blasphemy in the thought. That which is inhuman cannot be divine. Who can reason on such a proposition? They that can, may—I cannot. The time for such argument is past.

Name: _____ Date: _____

At a time like this, scorching irony, not convincing argument, is needed. Oh! had I the ability, and could I reach the nation's ear, I would today pour out a fiery stream of biting ridicule, blasting reproach, withering sarcasm, and stern rebuke. For it is not light that is needed, but fire; it is not the gentle shower, but thunder. We need the storm, the whirlwind, and the earthquake. The feeling of the nation must be quickened; the conscience of the nation must be roused; the propriety of the nation must be startled; the hypocrisy of the nation must be exposed; and its crimes against God and man must be denounced.

What to the American slave is your Fourth of July? I answer, a day that reveals to him more than all other days of the year, the gross injustice and cruelty to which he is the constant victim. To him your celebration is a sham; your boasted liberty an unholy license; your national greatness, swelling vanity; your sounds of rejoicing are empty and heartless; your shouts of liberty and equality, hollow mock; your prayers and hymns, your sermons and thanksgivings, with all your religious parade and solemnity, are to him mere bombast, fraud, deception, impiety, and hypocrisy—a thin veil to cover up crimes which would disgrace a nation of savages. There is not a nation of the earth guilty of practices more shocking and bloody than are the people of these United States at this very hour.

Go search where you will, roam through all the monarchies and despotisms of the Old World, travel through South America, search out every abuse and when you have found the last, lay your facts by the side of the everyday practices of this nation, and you will say with me that, for revolting barbarity and shameless hypocrisy, America reigns without a rival.

Handout 4.2

Blank Rhetorical Analysis Wheel

Directions: Draw arrows across elements to show connections.

Text: _____

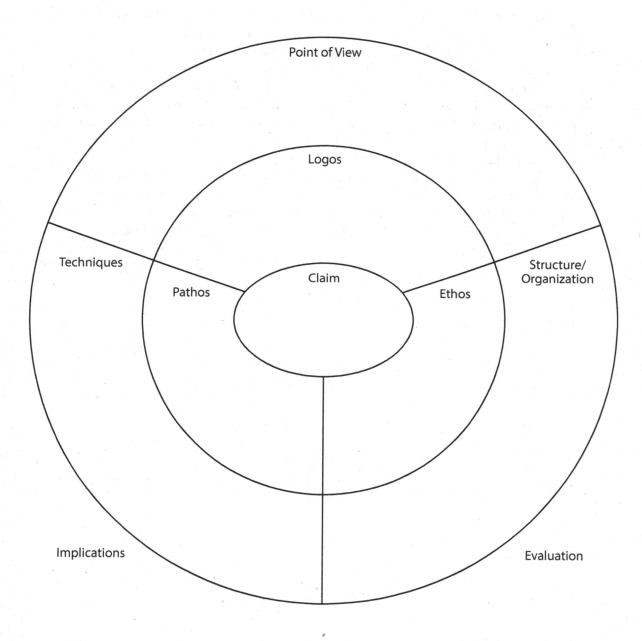

Created by Emily Mofield, Ed.D., & Tamra Stambaugh, Ph.D., 2015.

Handout 4.3
Freedom Chart

Text: _____	Text: _____	Text: _____
How would this author define freedom and whom it's for?		
What is the reason we must achieve this freedom?		
By what means must it be achieved?		
What will be the implications for achieving the freedom?		

Lesson

5

"First Inaugural Address"
by Abraham Lincoln

Goals/Objectives

Content: To analyze and interpret primary source texts, students will be able to:
- explain with evidence how a writer develops and supports a claim,
- respond to interpretations of historical speeches through a variety of contexts,
- compare and contrast various texts and real-world events on themes and generalizations, and
- evaluate rhetorical devices that influence effective argumentation within primary source documents.

Process: To develop thinking, writing, and communication, students will be able to:
- use evidence to develop appropriate inferences;
- evaluate use of effective argumentation;
- analyze primary sources (purpose, assumptions, consequences); and
- analyze societal or individual conflicts resulting from the struggle for freedom.

Concept: To understand the theme of freedom and related generalizations, students will be able to:
- support freedom generalizations with evidence from texts;
- apply inductive reasoning to develop generalizations relating to the concepts of freedom, security, individuals, diversity, equality, and democracy;
- describe external and internal threats to personal and national freedom; and
- examine definitions of freedom, means and motives for achieving freedom, and implications for freedom.

DOI: 10.4324/9781003235217-8

Materials

- "Map Showing the Distribution of the Slave Population of the Southern States," available at http://mappingthenation.com/index.php/viewer/index/4/1
- "First Reading of the Emancipation Proclamation of President Lincoln" (painting) by Francis Bicknell Carpenter, available at http://www.noaanews.noaa.gov/stories2011/images/cgs05195.jpg
- "Our National Bird" political cartoon from 1861 by Michael Angelo Woolf, available at http://hd.housedivided.dickinson.edu/node/21774
- Handout 5.1: Excerpts from "First Inaugural Address" by Abraham Lincoln
- Handout 5.2: Blank Rhetorical Analysis Wheel
- Rubric 1: Product Rubric (Appendix C)

Introductory Activities

1. Show "Map Showing the Distribution of the Slave Population of the Southern States," which was created from 1860 Census data. Ask students:
   - What general patterns do you notice about the slave population and geographic features?
   - Examine the slave population of where you live (or assign a state, such as Tennessee). What conclusions can you make based on the observations and patterns you see?
   - What surprises you about this map? What new questions do you have?
   - If you were Abraham Lincoln, how would you use this map?
   - If you were a Union general, how would you use this map?

2. Closely examine the painting, "First Reading of the Emancipation Proclamation of President Lincoln" by Francis Bicknell Carpenter. Ask:
   - What do you notice in the background?
   - Why might the map in the bottom right corner be an important part of decision making for Abraham Lincoln and his Cabinet members?
   - What do these documents reveal about the concept of unity?

3. Explain that students will be reading Lincoln's "First Inaugural Address," which was presented about a month before the Civil War. Ask: *What issues do you think Lincoln will address in his speech? What do you think his main claim will be?*

4. Before reading the text, explain that Aristotle categorized three branches of rhetoric—epideictic, deliberative, and forensic (explain that by contrast, logos, pathos, and ethos are *modes* of rhetoric):

- **Forensic rhetoric:** Involves discussing past action for purposes of accusing or defending (usually in legal situations).
- **Epideictic rhetoric:** Discusses present actions for the purpose of praise or blame; attempts to praise and/or blame ideas as good or bad (virtues or vices).
- **Deliberative rhetoric:** Discusses future actions for the purpose of convincing an audience to choose a course of action for the future.

Among scholars, there is much debate whether Lincoln's "First Inaugural Address" is primarily epideictic or deliberative. As students read, encourage them to consider which branch of rhetoric it most closely fits.

Text-Dependent Questions

Distribute Handout 5.1: "First Inaugural Address" by Abraham Lincoln. Allow students to read the text individually first. Then, read a paragraph at a time aloud, selecting from the following text-dependent questions to lead discussion.

- What can you infer about the attitudes of the Southern states toward Lincoln's election as president?
- How does Lincoln address the opposing perspective in the first paragraph? Why would he do this in his introduction of his Inaugural Address?
- Why does Lincoln refer to himself in third person? What appeal (i.e., ethos, logos, or pathos) is he employing in the first paragraph of the excerpt and why? (Sample response: Ethos—to build his credibility and trust the entire audience.)
- How does he support the idea that the Union is perpetual? How do we know what *perpetual* means from the context of the speech?
- Does Lincoln seem concerned about freeing slaves? What does he seem most concerned about?
- Does Lincoln appeal more to The Constitution or to the Union in developing his argument? (*Note:* This is likely very debatable.)
- Based on this document, what accusations can you infer have been put upon Lincoln?
- What word(s) does Lincoln use to refer to the United States throughout the document? How many times does he refer to it as "nation"? What does the term "Union" imply that "nation" does not? (Sample response: Lincoln refers to the U.S. as a Union; in subsequent speeches, he refers to it as a "nation.")
- When and how does Lincoln use analogy to develop his argument?
- What is the major problem in the speech? Does Lincoln offer a solution? How does Lincoln place responsibility on the listener and himself?

- Lincoln addresses opposition by saying, "If it were admitted that you who are dissatisfied hold the right side in the dispute, there still is no single good reason for precipitate action." Has Lincoln adequately supported that "there is still no good reason for precipitate action"?
- According to the last line, what is Lincoln implying by "mystic chords" and "chorus"? Who or what are the "better angels of our nature"?
- Is Lincoln successful in making an appeal to bind all Americans together? If so, how does he do this?
- Would you consider this speech primarily epideictic or deliberative? In what ways does it praise or blame? In what ways does it propose a course of action?

Rhetorical Analysis

Using Handout 5.2: Blank Rhetorical Analysis Wheel, guide students in analyzing how the author uses effective argumentation techniques. Students may take notes on the wheel and draw arrows to illustrate connections between elements. Sample questions and responses to lead the analysis include:

- **Context/Purpose:**
  - *What is the historical context?* President Abraham Lincoln presented this speech on March 4, 1861, as his First Inaugural Address. Between November 1860 and March 1861, seven Southern states had already seceded from the Union.
  - *What is Lincoln's purpose?* His goal is to present an argument for preserving the Union.

- **Claim:**
  - *What is Lincoln's main claim?* The Union is perpetual and must be preserved.

- **Point of View/Assumptions:**
  - *What is Lincoln's point of view and what are his assumptions?* Lincoln acknowledges his point of view as president that it is his job to preserve, protect, and defend the union. He assumes all authority is given to the Union, not individual states. He assumes others want him to address the issue of slavery, but he does not have the intention of doing so. He makes an assumption that the audience will be convicted of his religious appeals.

- **Logos/Technique/Structure:**
  - *How does Lincoln present his points? What techniques are used and how are his points organized?*

- ◆ **Logos/Reasoning:** He is not focused on interfering with slavery (addresses opposing point of view), establishes the problem, makes arguments for the perpetuity of the Union, puts ownership in the hands of the people, and concludes with analogy of mystic chords.
- ◆ **Techniques:** He establishes a deductive argument with an "if-then" statement ("but if destruction of the union . . . "), uses analogy and contrast of divorce (but notes the union cannot do this), and uses analogy of mystic chords as comparision to the unity of the nation.
- ◆ **Structure:** Problem-solution.

- ▪ **Pathos/Technique/Structure:**
  - *How does Lincoln develop emotional appeals?* He evokes conviction by referring to patriotism and religion ("Intelligence, patriotism, Christianity, and a firm reliance on Him . . . "), evokes a sense of duty and responsibility in the second to the last paragraph through contrast ("in your hands, not mine . . . "), and develops positive united feelings in the last paragraph by speaking about bonds of affection, patriots, every living heart, etc.

- ▪ **Ethos/Technique/Structure:**
  - *How does Lincoln develop credibility and trust?* At the beginning of the excerpt, he explains that his main concern is not about the institution of slavery. He consistently refers to the historical documents that established the Union and explains his duty as president is to defend and protect the Union.

- ▪ **Implications:**
  - *What are the implications/consequences of this speech?* This document highlights the importance of the Union and established reasons to not engage in Civil War.

- ▪ **Evaluation:**
  - *How effective is the author in supporting his claim?* Lincoln is effective in developing the argument that the Union must be preserved. He logically explains the Union itself is perpetual and cannot be destroyed of itself, uses exceptional ethos appeals in claiming his responsibility in preserving the Union, and evokes a sense of patriotism, responsibility, and unity among the people.

In-Class Activities to Deepen Learning

1. Ask: *To what extent do we still see implications of the division between the North and South today?* Consider evaluating interactive Electoral College maps from the past five elections. (*Note*: Students can go to http://www.270towin.com to access maps.) *What patterns do you notice? What inferences can we make?*

2. Show the political cartoon "Our National Bird, 1861" by Michael Angelo Woolf. Lead students through an analysis of the cartoon. Ask: *What is the main message of this cartoon? What is the point of view toward secession? What are the assumptions about Lincoln? What points of view are left out? What were the intended consequences of this cartoon? Based on Lincoln's speech, would he agree with the cartoon? Why or why not?*

Concept Connections

Guide students to understand how Lincoln's "First Inaugural Address" exemplifies freedom generalizations. Students should list examples about how the work demonstrates some of the generalizations. Lead students through a discussion using Handout 2.5: Concept Organizer. Figure 5.1 provides sample responses; various interpretations are encouraged. Note that in this lesson, the concept of *unity* is essential in preserving the democratic freedoms of the Constitution.

Choice-Based Differentiated Products

Students may choose one of the following as independent products to complete (*Note*: Use Rubric 1: Product Rubric in Appendix C to assess student products.):

- Examine a historical map relating to topics within this lesson. You may consider "Progress of Emancipation, 1850–1865" (available at http://etc.usf.edu/Maps/pages/2900/2978/2978z.htm). Complete a reflection using the following questions: What patterns do you notice? What is interesting about this map? What more do you want to learn after looking at this map? What does this reveal about *unity* of the United States? What inferences can you make about the relationship between geographical and political divisions by looking at the map? Explain your findings in a written reflection and present your findings in a class presentation.

- Read Abraham Lincoln's "Second Inaugural Address." Examine changes in Lincoln's tone and message in contrast to his "First Inaugural Address." Create a chart to contrast both speeches on his claims, purposes, tones, rhetorical techniques, and approaches to maintaining unity and democratic freedoms.

Freedom requires sacrifice.
Lincoln makes an argument to preserve the Union; he pleas for the dissatisfied countrymen to put aside their aggression to uphold the authority of the Union.
Freedom requires responsibility.
The opposition should not be an aggressor. To preserve the Union (and the freedoms/rights in the Constitution), we must not be enemies, but friends.
Freedom is threatened by internal and external forces.
Division (secession) is the main internal threat to preserving the Union and its freedoms.
Examine the relationship between freedom and another concept (e.g., power, conflict, change, order).
Lincoln called for putting aside conflict for the cause of preserving the Union (and all freedoms it upholds); put aside conflict to protect freedom.

Figure 5.1. Sample student responses.

- Imagine interviewing Lincoln a day before he takes office as president. Develop five questions to ask him related the historical context of the United States (e.g., "Mr. Lincoln, what are your main concerns when coming into office?"). Include at least one question related to freedom. Use knowledge from research and at least three pieces of evidence from the "First Inaugural Address" to provide answers from his perspective. Then, perform your interview in front of the class.

ELA Practice Tasks

Assign one of the following tasks as a performance-based assessment for this lesson:

- In an expository essay, explain how Lincoln's use of analogy in his "First Inaugural Address" is used to develop his argument. Cite at least two examples of analogy in your essay as well as any other relevant textual evidence.
- Create an argumentative essay with sufficient evidence from the text that answers the following question: Should Lincoln's "First Inaugural Address" be categorized as primarily epideictic or deliberative?

Social Studies Content Connections

Refer to the Social Studies Connection Wheel (see Appendix A for information and examples, and Appendix B for a Blank Social Studies Connection Wheel and Social Studies Connections Wheel Guide) to guide students in relating social stud-

	Inference from Evidence
0	Provides no response.
1	Response is limited, vague, and/or inaccurate. There is no justification for answers given.
2	Response is accurate, but lacks adequate explanation. Response includes some justification about the societal conflict.
3	Response is accurate and makes sense. Response includes some justification about the societal conflict.
4	Response is accurate, insightful, interpretive, and well written. Response includes thoughtful justification about the societal conflict.

Figure 5.2. Scoring guidelines for Lesson 5 formative assessment.

ies content to the text. The questions below focus on the historical context of the speech. The Big Idea Reflection: Primary Sources (Appendix B) can also be used to relate the text to historical content.

- **Text dependent:** What are the geographic and political influences on the problem addressed in Lincoln's speech?
- **Text dependent:** What does Lincoln mean when he says, "One of the declared objects for ordaining and establishing the Constitution was to form a more perfect union"? Which of the factors on the Social Studies Connections Wheel best matches this assertion? Explain.
- **Content dependent:** How did the nation's geography influence the economies of the North and the South? How did this interaction influence the conflict within the nation?

Formative Assessment

1. Ask students to respond to the following prompt in a single paragraph: *What is meant by "The Government will not assail you. You can have no conflict without being yourselves the aggressors. You have no oath registered in heaven to destroy the Government, while I shall have the most solemn one"? How does it relate to the societal conflict addressed?*
2. Use the scoring guidelines in Figure 5.2 to evaluate students' assessments.

Name: _____   Date: _____

Handout 5.1

Excerpts From "First Inaugural Address" *by Abraham Lincoln*

Delivered March 4, 1861

Fellow-Citizens of the United States:

. . . Apprehension seems to exist among the people of the Southern States that by the accession of a Republican Administration their property and their peace and personal security are to be endangered. There has never been any reasonable cause for such apprehension. Indeed, the most ample evidence to the contrary has all the while existed and been open to their inspection. It is found in nearly all the published speeches of him who now addresses you. I do but quote from one of those speeches when I declare that—

I have no purpose, directly or indirectly, to interfere with the institution of slavery in the States where it exists. I believe I have no lawful right to do so, and I have no inclination to do so.

Those who nominated and elected me did so with full knowledge that I had made this and many similar declarations and had never recanted them . . . .

It is seventy-two years since the first inauguration of a President under our National Constitution. During that period fifteen different and greatly distinguished citizens have in succession administered the executive branch of the Government. They have conducted it through many perils, and generally with great success. Yet, with all this scope of precedent, I now enter upon the same task for the brief constitutional term of four years under great and peculiar difficulty. A disruption of the Federal Union, heretofore only menaced, is now formidably attempted.

I hold that in contemplation of universal law and of the Constitution the Union of these States is perpetual. Perpetuity is implied, if not expressed, in the fundamental law of all national governments. It is safe to assert that no government proper ever had a provision in its organic law for its own termination. Continue to execute all the express provisions of our National Constitution, and the Union will endure forever, it being impossible to destroy it except by some action not provided for in the instrument itself . . . .

Descending from these general principles, we find the proposition that in legal contemplation the Union is perpetual confirmed by the history of the Union itself. The Union is much older than the Constitution. It was formed, in fact, by the Articles of Association in 1774. It was matured and continued by the Declaration of Independence in 1776. It was further matured, and the faith of all the then thirteen States expressly plighted and engaged that it should be perpetual, by the Articles of Confederation in 1778. And finally, in 1787, one of the declared objects for ordaining and establishing the Constitution was "to form a more perfect Union."

But if destruction of the Union by one or by a part only of the States be lawfully possible, the Union is less perfect than before the Constitution, having lost the vital element of perpetuity.

Handout 5.1, Continued

It follows from these views that no State upon its own mere motion can lawfully get out of the Union; that resolves and ordinances to that effect are legally void, and that acts of violence within any State or States against the authority of the United States are insurrectionary or revolutionary, according to circumstances.

I therefore consider that in view of the Constitution and the laws the Union is unbroken, and to the extent of my ability, I shall take care, as the Constitution itself expressly enjoins upon me, that the laws of the Union be faithfully executed in all the States. Doing this I deem to be only a simple duty on my part, and I shall perform it so far as practicable unless my rightful masters, the American people, shall withhold the requisite means or in some authoritative manner direct the contrary. I trust this will not be regarded as a menace, but only as the declared purpose of the Union that it will constitutionally defend and maintain itself . . . .

Physically speaking, we can not separate. We can not remove our respective sections from each other nor build an impassable wall between them. A husband and wife may be divorced and go out of the presence and beyond the reach of each other, but the different parts of our country can not do this . . . .

My countrymen, one and all, think calmly and well upon this whole subject. Nothing valuable can be lost by taking time. If there be an object to hurry any of you in hot haste to a step which you would never take deliberately, that object will be frustrated by taking time; but no good object can be frustrated by it. Such of you as are now dissatisfied still have the old Constitution unimpaired, and, on the sensitive point, the laws of your own framing under it; while the new Administration will have no immediate power, if it would, to change either. If it were admitted that you who are dissatisfied hold the right side in the dispute, there still is no single good reason for precipitate action. Intelligence, patriotism, Christianity, and a firm reliance on Him who has never yet forsaken this favored land are still competent to adjust in the best way all our present difficulty.

In your hands, my dissatisfied fellow-countrymen, and not in mine, is the momentous issue of civil war. The Government will not assail you. You can have no conflict without being yourselves the aggressors. You have no oath registered in heaven to destroy the Government, while I shall have the most solemn one to "preserve, protect, and defend it."

I am loath to close. We are not enemies, but friends. We must not be enemies. Though passion may have strained it must not break our bonds of affection. The mystic chords of memory, stretching from every battlefield and patriot grave to every living heart and hearthstone all over this broad land, will yet swell the chorus of the Union, when again touched, as surely they will be, by the better angels of our nature.

Name: _____ Date: _____

Handout 5.2
Blank Rhetorical Analysis Wheel

Directions: Draw arrows across elements to show connections.

Text: _____

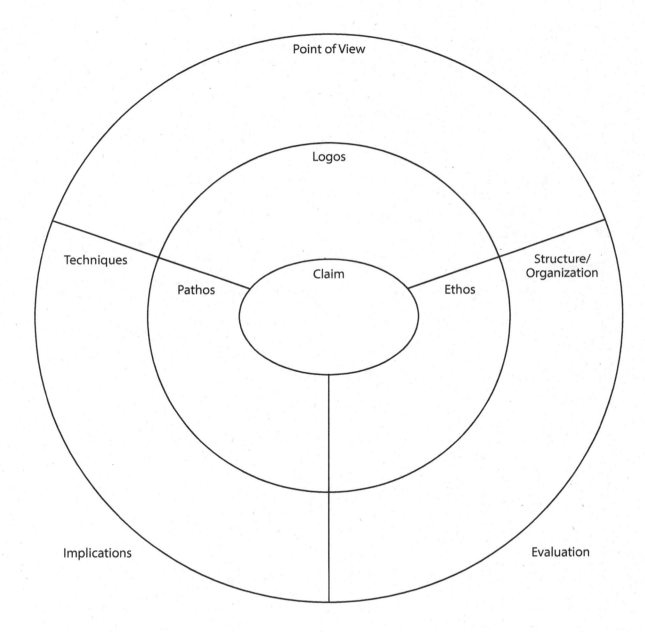

Purpose/Context

Point of View

Logos

Techniques

Structure/
Organization

Pathos

Claim

Ethos

Implications

Evaluation

Created by Emily Mofield, Ed.D., & Tamra Stambaugh, Ph.D., 2015.

Lesson

6

"Speech Before Congress"
by Carrie Chapman Catt

Goals/Objectives

Content: To analyze and interpret primary source texts, students will be able to:

- explain with evidence how a writer develops and supports a claim,
- respond to interpretations of historical speeches through a variety of contexts,
- compare and contrast various texts and real-world events on themes and generalizations, and
- evaluate rhetorical devices that influence effective argumentation within primary source documents.

Process: To develop thinking, writing, and communication, students will be able to:

- use evidence to develop appropriate inferences;
- evaluate use of effective argumentation;
- analyze primary sources (purpose, assumptions, consequences); and
- analyze societal or individual conflicts resulting from the struggle for freedom.

Concept: To understand the theme of freedom and related generalizations, students will be able to:

- support freedom generalizations with evidence from texts;
- apply inductive reasoning to develop generalizations relating to the concepts of freedom, security, individuals, diversity, equality, and democracy;
- describe external and internal threats to personal and national freedom; and
- examine definitions of freedom, means and motives for achieving freedom, and implications for freedom.

 DOI: 10.4324/9781003235217-9

Materials

- Political cartoons of Women's Suffrage Movement, early 1900s. We suggest using:
  - "Election Day" from 1909, available at http://www.loc.gov/pictures/item/97500226
  - "Stand Back Ladies" from January 28, 1911, from Votes for Women Broadside, Women's Political Union, available at http://memory.loc.gov/cgi-bin/query/h?ammem/rbcmillerbib:@field%28DOCID+@lit%28rbcmiller002522%29%29

- Carrie Chapman Catt's comments after women gained the right to vote on August 26, 1920, available at http://womenshistory.about.com/od/cattworks/a/womens_vote.htm
- Handout 6.1: "Speech Before Congress" by Carrie Chapman Catt
- Handout 6.2: Blank Rhetorical Analysis Wheel
- Rubric 1: Product Rubric (Appendix C)

Introductory Activities

1. Show students various political cartoons from the Women's Suffrage Movement of the early 1900s. We listed a couple of suggestions in the Materials section of this lesson. For the "Election Day" cartoon of 1909, ask students: *What is the main message of this cartoon? What is the cartoon's purpose? To whom is this directed? What are the prominent images and what could they represent? What else would you like to know about the image or historical context? What are the assumptions and implications?* You may also use the Big Idea Reflection for Primary Sources for a more in-depth discussion.

2. Show the political cartoon, "Stand Back Ladies," which was published January 28, 1911, by Votes for Women Broadside, Women's Political Union. Ask: *What is the main message of this cartoon? What is the cartoon's purpose? To whom is this directed? What are the prominent images and what could they represent? What else would you like to know about the image or historical context? What are the assumptions and implications?*

3. Provide brief background about the Women's Suffrage Movement of the early 1900s. You may also assign students to skim background information and present information to the class on the following suffragettes, suffrage organizations, and key players in the Women's Suffrage Movement:
   - Carrie Chapman Catt
   - Alice Stokes Paul

- Lucy Burns
- Silent Sentinels
- National American Woman Suffrage Association (NAWSA) and National Woman's Party (NWP). (Students may want to compare/contrast the organizations' methods and tactics.)
- Woodrow Wilson (Have students explain what his position toward women's suffrage was and why it changed.)
- The influence of World War I on the Women's Suffrage Movement

After presenting or hearing presentations, ask: *Was the National Woman's Party too extreme in its efforts? How were its efforts different from those of the NAWSA? Did some methods work better than others?*

1. Explain that the Silent Sentinels held banners in front of the White House. Russian envoys were visiting the White House in 1917. Banners read, "To the Russian envoys: We the women of America tell you that America is not a democracy. Twenty million American women are denied the right to vote. President Wilson is the chief opponent of their national enfranchisement . . . Tell our government it must liberate its people before it can claim free Russia as an ally."

2. **Engage students in a quick debate.** Students may stand on opposite sides of the room based on their answers. Ask: *Do you agree with this sentiment? Was America a democracy? What is the definition of democracy? How might opponents against women's suffrage argue America is in fact a democracy, even though women are not represented?* Emphasize that women were absolutely powerless in changing legislation because they could not vote to change it. Unless they could convince men to vote for their point of view, women could not be represented.

Text-Dependent Questions

Distribute Handout 6.1: "Speech Before Congress" by Carrie Chapman Catt. Explain that this speech was given at a time when the Women's Suffrage Movement had contrasting views about how to approach gaining equal freedoms. Carrie Chapman Catt was more conservative than Lucy Burns and Alice Stokes Paul were. Allow students to read the text individually first. Then, read a paragraph at a time aloud, selecting from the following text-dependent questions to lead discussion.

- How does the mentioning of "taxation without representation" relate to her argument?
- What paradoxes does Catt reveal in her development of argument? (Note her expressions about the nation being hypocritical about democracy.)

- Based on her reasoning in the text, would Catt argue that the United States is a democracy?
- Why does Catt include the quote from Elihu Root, "The world cannot be half democratic and half autocratic. It must be all democratic or all Prussian"? How is she applying it to support her second point that women suffrage is inevitable?
- Catt asks four rhetorical questions, such as "Do you realize statements?" Which one is most powerful? Why?
- What exactly does Catt want Congress to do? When she asks, "Can you afford the risk?," what is exactly is the "risk"?
- This speech is often titled, "The Woman's Hour is Struck," based on Catt's statement in the speech. Is this an appropriate title for the speech? Would other phrases from the speech be more appropriate? If so, what?
- How does Catt develop a sense of urgency in her speech?
- Why does she end her speech with a question? What impact would this have on the individuals in Congress? (Sample response: It encourages the audience to reflect.)
- How does Catt logically structure her argument, inductively or deductively? How do you know? (Sample response: Deductively; she starts with her premise "women's suffrage is inevitable" and supports it.)
- What moments are most compelling in the speech?
- What connections can you make with this text and the texts previously studied in this unit (e.g., the ones by Patrick Henry, Frederick Douglass, Abraham Lincoln)? How is her argument similar to other previously studied text? (*Note*: Help students see the connection of hypocrisy in Douglass's speech and liberty in Patrick Henry's speech.)

Rhetorical Analysis

Using Handout 6.2: Blank Rhetorical Analysis Wheel, guide students in analyzing how the author uses effective argumentation techniques. Students may take notes on the wheel and draw arrows to illustrate connections between elements. Sample questions and responses to lead the analysis include:

- **Context/Purpose:**
  - *What is the historical context?* Catt presented this speech in 1917 to Congress.
  - *What is Catt's purpose?* Her goal is to argue for the passage of an amendment for women's suffrage.

- **Claim:**
  - *What is Catt's main claim?* It is time for women's suffrage to be a reality in the U.S.

- **Point of View/Assumptions:**
  - *What is Catt's point of view? What assumptions does she question?* Catt advocates for women's suffrage; she questions the assumptions that democracy is only for men.

- **Logos/Technique/Structure:**
  - *How does Catt present her points? What techniques are used and how are her points organized?*
    - ◆ **Logos/Reasoning:** She establishes her thesis (women's suffrage is inevitable) and supports it with three clearly established points.
    - ◆ **Techniques:** She uses the analogy of "taxation without representation" to point out hypocrisy of the U.S., presents the fact that professional women cannot vote, and uses an Elihu Root quote to apply to the U.S.
    - ◆ **Structure:** Point by point. She explains three reasons why women's suffrage is inevitable.

- **Pathos/Technique/Structure:**
  - *How does Catt develop emotional appeals?* Her repetition of rhetorical questions evokes conviction and guilt; her accusatory tone toward America's democracy evokes conviction. She establishes a sense of urgency by saying "the woman's hour has struck" and addresses various groups of Congress separately at the end to evoke emotion in each group.

- **Ethos/Technique/Structure:**
  - *How does Catt develop credibility and trust?* She cites Lincoln and Wilson in proclaiming the principles of democracy, and cites the Declaration of Independence and Elihu Root to establish credibility.

- **Implications:**
  - *What are the implications/consequences of this speech?* Congress passed the 19th Amendment on June 4, 1919.

- **Evaluation:**
  - *How effective is the author in supporting her claim?* Catt effectively uses logos, pathos, and ethos appeals to develop her argument (supported from above evidence).

In-Class Activities to Deepen Learning

1. Explain to students that Catt sometimes used prejudice appeals to convince others of voting for women's suffrage. For example, when trying to persuade Mississippi and South Carolina, she argued that White supremacy would be strengthened by women's suffrage. Ask: *In your opinion, is Catt being hypocritical in her approach to win women suffrage votes? There has been a controversy whether Catt deserves to be honored for her work (e.g., such as having university buildings named after her) because of this issue. Does she deserve to be honored?*

2. End the lesson by reading aloud Carrie Chapman Catt's comments given on August 26, 1920, celebrating winning the vote for women (available at http://womenshistory.about.com/od/cattworks/a/womens_vote.htm). Consider asking a student to read it passionately. Ask: *What is the most powerful phrase or sentence in this speech, and why? How does this speech relate to the generalization "freedom requires sacrifice"?*

Concept Connections

Guide students to understand how Catt's speech before Congress exemplifies freedom generalizations. Students should list examples about how the speech demonstrates some of the generalizations. Use Handout 2.5: Concept Organizer to help students organize their thoughts. Provide guidance as needed. Figure 6.1 provides some sample responses.

Choice-Based Differentiated Products

Students may choose one of the following as independent products to complete (*Note*: Use Rubric 1: Product Rubric in Appendix C to assess student products.):

- Examine a map showing the dates states achieved women's suffrage. What patterns do you notice about the timeline of women's suffrage and geography? What ideals may have influenced the thinking in the geographic regions? Support your answer citing evidence from relevant research.
- Read a chapter from the book *Jailed for Freedom* by Doris Stevens. Free access to this eBook is available online. This book includes details about the experiences of Lucy Burns and other suffragists who went to jail for their protests. After reading, write a reflection by minimally answering the following questions: What challenges were encountered? What new insight is revealed about the motivations of the women? What is the most interesting aspect you read about and why? How does the experience you read about related to another issue you have studied? After reading this text,

Freedom requires sacrifice.
The members of Congress may face opposition from "women haters" and "old males of the tribe" if they vote for a Constitutional amendment.
Freedom requires responsibility.
Catt asserts that it is the responsibility for Congress to uphold the democratic ideals proclaimed by America (e.g., voice in own government, rebelling against taxation without representation).
Freedom is threatened by internal and external forces.
Freedom for women to vote is threatened by internal forces in Congress.
Examine the relationship between freedom and another concept (e.g., power, conflict, change, order).
Catt asserts that the ideal of democracy is freedom for all.

Figure 6.1. Sample student responses.

how would you respond to the claim that studying the Women's Suffrage Movement is not necessary today? How does this text make you think about yourself and the world differently?

- Research more details about the Night of Terror (November 14 or 15, 1917; the date is debatable). After reading details about the experiences of the suffragettes in jail, write a newspaper article or newspaper editorial about these experiences (write from the year 1917). Relate the content of your article to a freedom generalization.

- Examine at least five women's suffrage political cartoons. Develop a visual (e.g., poster, Prezi, PowerPoint, etc.) to show the class. Explain the message, audience, purpose, context, techniques, prominent images, emotions, and implications of each cartoon.

- Read the lyrics to at least five suffragist songs or poems. After reading all five, choose one to examine closely. Reflect on the following questions: What argument about suffrage does it mainly address? How does the author appeal to women? In what ways are repeated words and phrases important? Develop an illustration or political cartoon to accompany the lyrics of the song. Present the lyrics, your reflection, and illustration to the class.

ELA Practice Task

Assign the following task as a performance-based assessment for this lesson: *Compare Carrie Chapman Catt's speech to Frederick Douglass's speech (from Lesson 4). How do they use similar techniques to develop their arguments? Explain your answer in a well-developed essay.*

98

Inference from Evidence	
0	Provides no response.
1	Response is limited, vague, and/or inaccurate. There is no justification for answers given.
2	Response is accurate, but lacks adequate explanation. Response includes some justification about the societal conflict.
3	Response is accurate and makes sense. Response includes some justification about the societal conflict.
4	Response is accurate, insightful, interpretive, and well written. Response includes thoughtful justification about the societal conflict.

Figure 6.2. Scoring guidelines for Lesson 6 formative assessment.

Social Studies Content Connections

Refer to the Social Studies Connection Wheel (see Appendix A for information and examples, and Appendix B for a Blank Social Studies Connection Wheel and Social Studies Connections Wheel Guide) to guide students in relating social studies content to the text. The questions below focus on the historical context of the speech. The Big Idea Reflection: Primary Sources (Appendix B) can also be used to relate the text to historical content.

- **Content dependent:** How did industrialization contribute to social factors influencing the Women's Suffrage Movement?
- **Content dependent:** How was the Temperance Movement and Pro-Abolitionist Movement influential on women's suffrage?
- **Text dependent:** What social studies factors interact to create the problem addressed in Catt's speech?
- **Content dependent:** What were consequences of the 19th Amendment on women's suffrage movements across the world?

Formative Assessment

1. Ask students to respond to the following prompt in a single paragraph: *What can you infer is meant by "Behold our Uncle Sam floating the banner with one hand, 'Taxation without representation is tyranny,' and with the other seizing the billions of dollars paid in taxes by women to whom he refuses 'representation'"? What does this quote reveal about the societal conflict addressed in the speech?*
2. Use the scoring guidelines in Figure 6.2 to evaluate students' assessments.

Handout 6.1

"Speech Before Congress" *by Carrie Chapman Catt*

Delivered November 4, 1917

Woman suffrage is inevitable. Suffragists knew it before November 4, 1917; opponents afterward. Three distinct causes made it inevitable.

First, the history of our country. Ours is a nation born of revolution, of rebellion against a system of government so securely entrenched in the customs and traditions of human society that in 1776 it seemed impregnable. From the beginning of things, nations had been ruled by kings and for kings, while the people served and paid the cost. The American Revolutionists boldly proclaimed the heresies: "Taxation without representation is tyranny." "Governments derive their just powers from the consent of the governed." The colonists won, and the nation which was established as a result of their victory has held unfailingly that these two fundamental principles of democratic government are not only the spiritual source of our national existence but have been our chief historic pride and at all times the sheet anchor of our liberties.

Eighty years after the Revolution, Abraham Lincoln welded those two maxims into a new one: "Ours is a government of the people, by the people, and for the people." Fifty years more passed and the president of the United States, Woodrow Wilson, in a mighty crisis of the nation, proclaimed to the world: "We are fighting for the things which we have always carried nearest to our hearts: for democracy, for the right of those who submit to authority to have a voice in their own government."

All the way between these immortal aphorisms political leaders have declared unabated faith in their truth. Not one American has arisen to question their logic in the 141 years of our national existence. However stupidly our country may have evaded the logical application at times, it has never swerved from its devotion to the theory of democracy as expressed by those two axioms . . .

With such a history behind it, how can our nation escape the logic it has never failed to follow, when its last unenfranchised class calls for the vote? Behold our Uncle Sam floating the banner with one hand, "Taxation without representation is tyranny," and with the other seizing the billions of dollars paid in taxes by women to whom he refuses "representation." Behold him again, welcoming the boys of twenty-one and the newly made immigrant citizen to "a voice in their own government" while he denies that fundamental right of democracy to thousands of women public school teachers from whom many of these men learn all they know of citizenship and patriotism, to women college presidents, to women who preach in our pulpits, interpret law in our courts, preside over our hospitals, write books and magazines, and serve in every uplifting moral and social enterprise. Is there a single man who can justify such inequality of treatment, such outrageous discrimination? Not one . . .

Second, the suffrage for women already established in the United States makes women suffrage for the nation inevitable. When Elihu Root, as president of the American Society

Handout 6.1, Continued

of International Law, at the eleventh annual meeting in Washington, April 26, 1917, said, "The world cannot be half democratic and half autocratic. It must be all democratic or all Prussian. There can be no compromise," he voiced a general truth. Precisely the same intuition has already taught the blindest and most hostile foe of woman suffrage that our nation cannot long continue a condition under which government in half its territory rests upon the consent of half of the people and in the other half upon the consent of all the people; a condition which grants representation to the taxed in half of its territory and denies it in the other half a condition which permits women in some states to share in the election of the president, senators, and representatives and denies them that privilege in others. It is too obvious to require demonstration that woman suffrage, now covering half our territory, will eventually be ordained in all the nation. No one will deny it. The only question left is when and how will it be completely established.

Third, the leadership of the United States in world democracy compels the enfranchisement of its own women. The maxims of the Declaration were once called "fundamental principles of government." They are now called "American principles" or even "Americanisms." They have become the slogans of every movement toward political liberty the world around, of every effort to widen the suffrage for men or women in any land. Not a people, race, or class striving for freedom is there anywhere in the world that has not made our axioms the chief weapon of the struggle. More, all men and women the world around, with farsighted vision into the verities of things, know that the world tragedy of our day is not now being waged over the assassination of an archduke, nor commercial competition, nor national ambitions, nor the freedom of the seas. It is a death grapple between the forces which deny and those which uphold the truths of the Declaration of Independence . . .

Do you realize that in no other country in the world with democratic tendencies is suffrage so completely denied as in a considerable number of our own states? There are thirteen black states where no suffrage for women exists, and fourteen others where suffrage for women is more limited than in many foreign countries.

Do you realize that when you ask women to take their cause to state referendum you compel them to do this: that you drive women of education, refinement, achievement, to beg men who cannot read for their political freedom?

Do you realize that such anomalies as a college president asking her janitor to give her a vote are overstraining the patience and driving women to desperation?

Do you realize that women in increasing numbers indignantly resent the long delay in their enfranchisement?

Your party platforms have pledged women suffrage. Then why not be honest, frank friends of our cause, adopt it in reality as your own, make it a party program, and "fight with us"? As a party measure—a measure of all parties—why not put the amendment through Congress and the legislatures? We shall all be better friends, we shall have a happier nation, we women will be free to support loyally the party of our choice, and we shall be far prouder of our history.

"There is one thing mightier than kings and armies"—aye, than Congresses and political parties—"the power of an idea when its time has come to move." The time for woman suffrage has come. The woman's hour has struck. If parties prefer to postpone action longer and thus do battle with this idea, they challenge the inevitable. The idea will not perish; the party which opposes it may. Every delay, every trick, every political dishonesty from now on will antagonize the women of the land more and more, and when the party or parties which have so delayed woman suffrage finally let it come, their sincerity will be doubted and their appeal to the new voters will be met with suspicion. This is the psychology of the situation. Can you afford the risk? Think it over . . .

To you and the supporters of our cause in Senate and House, and the number is large, the suffragists of the nation express their grateful thanks. This address is not meant for you. We are more truly appreciative of all you have done than any words can express. We ask you to make a last, hard fight for the amendment during the present session. Since last we asked a vote on this amendment, your position has been fortified by the addition to suffrage territory of Great Britain, Canada, and New York.

Some of you have been too indifferent to give more than casual attention to this question. It is worthy of your immediate consideration. A question big enough to engage the attention of our allies in wartime is too big a question for you to neglect.

Some of you have grown old in party service. Are you willing that those who take your places by and by shall blame you for having failed to keep pace with the world and thus having lost for them a party advantage? Is there any real gain for you, for your party, for your nation by delay? Do you want to drive the progressive men and women out of your party?

Some of you hold to the doctrine of states' rights as applying to woman suffrage. Adherence to that theory will keep the United States far behind all other democratic nations upon this question. A theory which prevents a nation from keeping up with the trend of world progress cannot be justified.

Gentlemen, we hereby petition you, our only designated representatives, to redress our grievances by the immediate passage of the Federal Suffrage Amendment and to use your influence to secure its ratification in your own state, in order that the women of our nation may be endowed with political freedom before the next presidential election, and that our nation may resume its world leadership in democracy.

Woman suffrage is coming—you know it. Will you, Honorable Senators and Members of the House of Representatives, help or hinder it?

Handout 6.2
Blank Rhetorical Analysis Wheel _____

Directions: Draw arrows across elements to show connections.

Text: _____

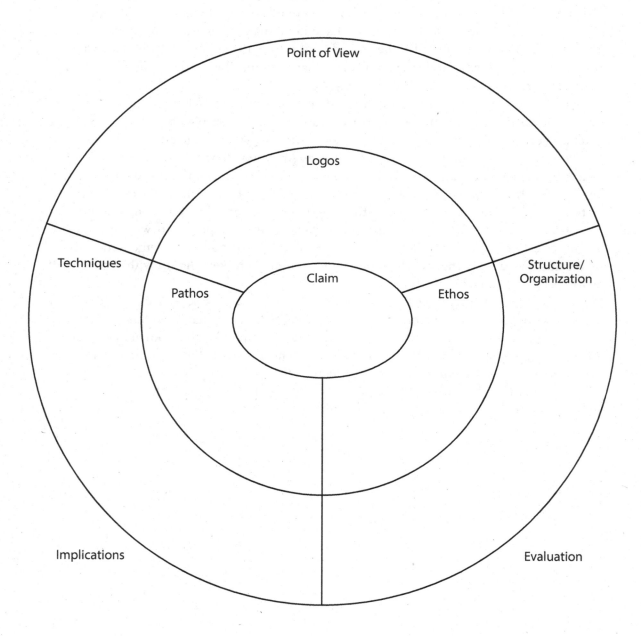

Purpose/Context

Point of View

Logos

Techniques

Pathos   Claim   Ethos

Structure/
Organization

Implications

Evaluation

Created by Emily Mofield, Ed.D., & Tamra Stambaugh, Ph.D., 2015.

Lesson

7

"A Day of Infamy"
by Franklin D. Roosevelt

Goals/Objectives

Content: To analyze and interpret primary source texts, students will be able to:
- explain with evidence how a writer develops and supports a claim,
- respond to interpretations of historical speeches through a variety of contexts,
- compare and contrast various texts and real-world events on themes and generalizations, and
- evaluate rhetorical devices that influence effective argumentation within primary source documents.

Process: To develop thinking, writing, and communication, students will be able to:
- use evidence to develop appropriate inferences;
- evaluate use of effective argumentation;
- analyze primary sources (purpose, assumptions, consequences); and
- analyze societal or individual conflicts resulting from the struggle for freedom.

Concept: To understand the theme of freedom and related generalizations, students will be able to:
- support freedom generalizations with evidence from texts;
- apply inductive reasoning to develop generalizations relating to the concepts of freedom, security, individuals, diversity, equality, and democracy;
- describe external and internal threats to personal and national freedom; and
- examine definitions of freedom, means and motives for achieving freedom, and implications for freedom.

 DOI: 10.4324/9781003235217-10

Materials

- Small-group copies of excerpts from various documents (retrieved online). We suggest:
  - James K. Polk's declaration of war against Mexico, May 11, 1846, available at http://www.dmwv.org/mexwar/docs/polk.htm
  - President Woodrow Wilson's "War Message," April 2, 1917, available at http://wwi.lib.byu.edu/index.php/Wilson%27s_War_Message_to_Congress
  - German Declaration of War Against the United States, December 11, 1941, by Adolf Hitler, available at http://www.ihr.org/jhr/v08/v08p389_Hitler.html
  - Lyndon B. Johnson's "Report on the Gulf of Tonkin Incident," August 4, 1964, available at http://www.millercenter.org/the-presidency/presidential-speeches/august-4-1964-report-gulf-tonkin-incident

- Handout 4.3: Freedom Chart
- Handout 7.1: "A Day of Infamy" by Franklin D. Roosevelt
- Handout 7.2: Blank Rhetorical Analysis Wheel
- Rubric 1: Product Rubric (Appendix C)

Introductory Activity

Engage students in a quick debate. Ask students to stand on opposite sides of the room (yes vs. no) and discuss their opinions on the following questions:

- Is war a necessary evil? Yes or No? Why?
- Is war needed to establish peace? Yes or No? Why?

Text-Dependent Questions

Distribute Handout 7.1: "A Day of Infamy" by Franklin D. Roosevelt. Allow students to read the text individually first, or you may allow them to listen to an audio version of the speech (accessible online). Then, read a paragraph at a time aloud, selecting from the following text-dependent questions to lead discussion.

- Roosevelt opens with the famous line ". . . a date which will live in infamy." What is implied by "infamy"? How is it different from "fame," "renown," or "notoriety"?
- Why does Roosevelt make a point that the United States was at peace with Japan?

- Closely examine the paragraph beginning with "It will be recorded that the distance . . . " What words are used to evoke an emotional reaction in the audience?
- How does repetition enhance Roosevelt's message? Is it used for emphasis, clarity, or emotional impact?
- What do you notice about his sentence structure compared to other speeches read in this unit? Why do you think he takes this approach, and what effect does it have on his argument? (Sample response: It is much shorter and matter-of-fact, direct and simple, helping the audience to understand the Japanese attacked U.S.)
- What assumptions does Roosevelt have about his audience and the people of the United States?
- As you read the remainder of the document, note Roosevelt's word choice. What particular words and phrases evoke fear? Which words evoke patriotic feelings?
- Identify instances when Roosevelt uses absolutes (e.g., always, no, never, certain). Why is this an effective technique in developing his argument?
- How do Roosevelt's style and rhetorical techniques compare to Madison's style and techniques in "Proclamation Upon British Depredations, Burning of the Capitol" (Lesson 2)?

Rhetorical Analysis

Using Handout 7.2: Blank Rhetorical Analysis Wheel, guide students in analyzing how the author uses effective argumentation techniques. Students may take notes on the wheel and draw arrows to illustrate connections between elements. Sample questions and responses to lead the analysis include:

- **Context/Purpose:**
  - *What is the historical context?* Roosevelt presented this speech to Congress on December 8, 1941, as a response to the attacks at Pearl Harbor.
  - *What is Roosevelt's purpose?* His goal is to declare war and explain why.

- **Claim:**
  - *What is Roosevelt's main claim?* Because Japan has attacked Pearl Harbor, the U.S. will go to war with Japan.

- **Point of View/Assumptions:**
  - *What is Roosevelt's point of view? What assumptions does he make?* As president, he is speaking from a point of view to protect and defend the

nation. He makes the assumption that the American people will agree war is necessary and will win through victory.

- ▪ **Logos/Technique/Structure:**
  - *How does Roosevelt use logic to present his points? What techniques are used and how are his points organized?*
    - ◆ **Logos/Reasoning:** He presents facts that this was a surprise attack during a time when peaceful negotiations were attempted, presents facts of Pacific area attacks, presents hope of victory, and declares war.
    - ◆ **Techniques:** He cites facts/evidence of Japanese attacks and the causes of the attacks (damage to naval and military forces), and uses repetition of "deliberate" and "last night."
    - ◆ **Structure:** Problem-solution.

- ▪ **Pathos/Technique/Structure:**
  - *How does Roosevelt develop emotional appeals?* He uses "infamy" to create negative connotation, develops negative emotions toward enemy through loaded language and repetition, and evokes sense of hope and determination through positive language (e.g., "righteous might," "absolute victory," "unbounding determination," etc.).

- ▪ **Ethos/Technique/Structure:**
  - *How does Roosevelt develop credibility and trust?* He addresses the fact that the U.S. tried peaceful negotiations to no avail and cites himself as commander in chief as he begins to describe the solution.

- ▪ **Implications:**
  - *What are the implications/consequenes of this speech?* The U.S. becomes involved in WWII.

- ▪ **Evaluation:**
  - *How effective is the author in supporting his claim?* Roosevelt gives substantial reasons for going to war with Japan.

In-Class Activities to Deepen Learning

1. Introduce Ronald Reid's (1997) framework for understanding prowar rhetoric. These are methods used to convince an audience that war is necessary.
   - ▪ **Territorial appeal:** Persuades the audience that the land must be protected. The land is being threatened, and we must "defend" it. The audi-

ence is likely to accept war more as a defensive act than an offensive one. In addition, it appeals to the idea of expansionism and the notion of reclaiming territory that was wrongfully taken away.

- **Ethnocentric appeal:** Creates an "us versus them" mentality by believing one culture is better than another. This is achieved through emotional intensity—describing the enemy as barbaric, animalistic, savage-like, or violent. God is on the side of the superior culture, or the opposition poses a cultural threat (e.g., barbarism versus gallantry).
- **Optimistic appeal:** Creates an idea that war is only positive. This creates a sense of hope, and the audience believes winning the war will be inevitable.

More information can be found about these appeals by doing a simple search online for "Ronald Reid prowar rhetoric." Ask students to go back through Roosevelt's speech and find examples of these appeals. These might be considered part of "pathos" appeals or simply techniques.

1. Pass out excerpts from other declarations of war to groups of students (see suggestions in the Materials section at the beginning of this lesson). Students should underline/highlight the types of Reid's prowar rhetoric within the text. Assigning small excerpts are acceptable because some of these are rather lengthy documents. Allow groups to share their findings with the class. Emphasize similarities between groups.
2. Ask students to write a letter to an aged war veteran (consider World War II, Korean War, Vietnam, etc.), expressing gratitude to him or her for defending freedom. Mail your letter to an organization that coordinates U.S. veteran honor flights (e.g., The Honor Flight Network). Many of these organizations deliver letters to veterans as part of their service.

Concept Connections

1. Ask students: *How does war relate to freedom?* Figure 7.1 provides some sample responses that may be helpful in guiding students to understand how the lesson relates to freedom generalizations. Students record their reflections on Handout 2.5: Concept Organizer, continued from previous lessons.
2. Have students complete Handout 4.3: Freedom Chart to further examine concept connections.

Choice-Based Differentiated Products

Students may choose one of the following as independent products to complete (*Note*: Use Rubric 1: Product Rubric in Appendix C to assess student products.):

Freedom requires sacrifice.
Roosevelt argues that in order to protect the freedoms of the U.S., the U.S. must go to war with Japan. America's interests are in "grave danger" unless the sacrifice of war is made.
Freedom requires responsibility.
Roosevelt asserts that Congress must take responsibility and declare war in order to protect America's interests.
Freedom is threatened by internal and external forces.
Freedom is threatened by the external force of the Japanese attack on Pearl Harbor.
Examine the relationship between freedom and another concept (e.g., power, conflict, change, order).
Students may examine the relationship between defense, freedom, power, response, and other concepts.

Figure 7.1. Sample student responses.

- In a chart, compare Franklin D. Roosevelt's "A Day of Infamy" to James Madison's "Proclamation Upon British Depredations" from Lesson 2. Cite at least four pieces of textual evidence in your comparison, specifically relating to how they use similar approaches in developing their arguments. Consider Reid's prowar rhetorical appeals in analyzing the similarities. A sample chart is provided in Figure 7.2.
- Is war needed to establish peace? Many argue that with power comes responsibility, but is it the United States' responsibility to establish democracy in other parts of the world where it is not welcome? Still, others argue that a threat to democracy somewhere is a threat to democracy everywhere. After researching this topic, examine both sides of the issue and present the arguments to the class.
- Write an editorial essay to defend why the U.S. should or should not stay in a current war or participate in a potential war (depending on current issue). Relate to a freedom generalization in your editorial.

ELA Practice Task

Assign the following task as a performance-based assessment for this lesson: *Write a review that analyzes the strengths and weaknesses of Franklin D. Roosevelt's arguments for war. Consider what is included in the speech and what is left out. Cite relevant textual examples in your review.*

Roosevelt's Text (1941)	Similarities in argument	Madison's Text (1814)

Figure 7.2. Sample chart for comparing Roosevelt's "A Day of Infamy" to Madison's "Proclamation Upon British Depredations."

Social Studies Content Connections

Refer to the Social Studies Connection Wheel (see Appendix A for information and examples, and Appendix B for a Blank Social Studies Connection Wheel and Social Studies Connections Wheel Guide) to guide students in relating social studies content to the text. The questions below focus on the historical context of the speech. The Big Idea Reflection: Primary Sources (Appendix B) can also be used to relate the text to historical content.

- **Content dependent:** Explain the influence of geography and politics on the relationship between Japan and the U.S. How did the overall world context contribute to the conflict?
- **Text dependent:** How are the concepts of power and conflict addressed within Roosevelt's speech?
- **Content-dependent:** What made the attack on Pearl Harbor significant for both Japan and the U.S.? Explain your answer using at least two factors from the Social Studies Connections Wheel.

Formative Assessment

1. Ask students to respond to the following prompt in a single paragraph: *How effective is Franklin D. Roosevelt in developing his argument? Support your answer by referring to elements of effective argumentation.*
2. Use the scoring guidelines in Figure 7.3 to evaluate students' assessments.

Effective Rhetoric	
0	Provides no response.
1	Response is limited and vague. Response only partially answers the question. A rhetorical element is not mentioned.
2	Response is accurate with one to two rhetorical elements named. Response includes limited or no evidence from text. OR Response includes evidence from text, but does not relate to a rhetorical element.
3	Response is appropriate and accurate, describing one to two rhetorical elements to support effective argumentation. Response includes some evidence from the text.
4	Response is insightful and well supported, describing two to three rhetorical elements. Response includes evidence from the text.

Figure 7.3. Scoring guidelines for Lesson 7 formative assessment.

Handout 7.1

"A Day of Infamy" *by Franklin D. Roosevelt*

Delivered December 8, 1941

Yesterday, Dec. 7, 1941—a date which will live in infamy—the United States of America was suddenly and deliberately attacked by naval and air forces of the Empire of Japan.

The United States was at peace with that nation and, at the solicitation of Japan, was still in conversation with the government and its emperor looking toward the maintenance of peace in the Pacific.

Indeed, one hour after Japanese air squadrons had commenced bombing in Oahu, the Japanese ambassador to the United States and his colleagues delivered to the Secretary of State a formal reply to a recent American message. While this reply stated that it seemed useless to continue the existing diplomatic negotiations, it contained no threat or hint of war or armed attack.

It will be recorded that the distance of Hawaii from Japan makes it obvious that the attack was deliberately planned many days or even weeks ago. During the intervening time, the Japanese government has deliberately sought to deceive the United States by false statements and expressions of hope for continued peace.

The attack yesterday on the Hawaiian islands has caused severe damage to American naval and military forces. Very many American lives have been lost. In addition, American ships have been reported torpedoed on the high seas between San Francisco and Honolulu.

Yesterday, the Japanese government also launched an attack against Malaya.

Last night, Japanese forces attacked Hong Kong.

Last night, Japanese forces attacked Guam.

Last night, Japanese forces attacked the Philippine Islands.

Last night, the Japanese attacked Wake Island.

This morning, the Japanese attacked Midway Island.

Japan has, therefore, undertaken a surprise offensive extending throughout the Pacific area. The facts of yesterday speak for themselves. The people of the United States have already formed their opinions and well understand the implications to the very life and safety of our nation.

As commander in chief of the Army and Navy, I have directed that all measures be taken for our defense.

Always will we remember the character of the onslaught against us.

No matter how long it may take us to overcome this premeditated invasion, the American people in their righteous might will win through to absolute victory.

I believe I interpret the will of the Congress and of the people when I assert that we will not only defend ourselves to the uttermost, but will make very certain that this form of treachery shall never endanger us again.

Name: _____ **Date:** _____

Handout 7.1, Continued
_____

Hostilities exist. There is no blinking at the fact that our people, our territory and our interests are in grave danger.

With confidence in our armed forces—with the unbounding determination of our people—we will gain the inevitable triumph—so help us God.

I ask that the Congress declare that since the unprovoked and dastardly attack by Japan on Sunday, Dec. 7, a state of war has existed between the United States and the Japanese empire.

Name: _____ Date: _____

Handout 7.2
Blank Rhetorical Analysis Wheel

Directions: Draw arrows across elements to show connections.

Text: _____

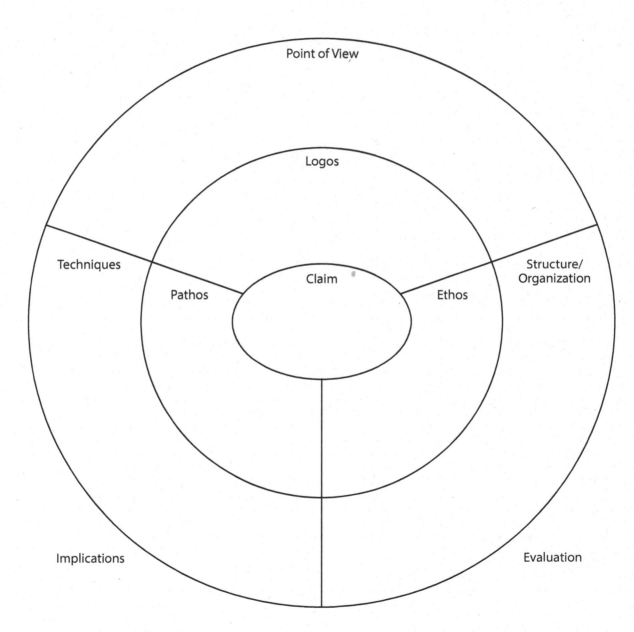

Purpose/Context

Point of View

Logos

Techniques

Pathos

Claim

Ethos

Structure/Organization

Implications

Evaluation

Created by Emily Mofield, Ed.D., & Tamra Stambaugh, Ph.D., 2015.

Lesson

8

"Special Message to Congress on Urgent National Needs—Space"
by John F. Kennedy

Goals/Objectives

Content: To analyze and interpret primary source texts, students will be able to:
- explain with evidence how a writer develops and supports a claim,
- respond to interpretations of historical speeches through a variety of contexts,
- compare and contrast various texts and real-world events on themes and generalizations, and
- evaluate rhetorical devices that influence effective argumentation within primary source documents.

Process: To develop thinking, writing, and communication, students will be able to:
- reason through an issue by analyzing points of view, assumptions, and implications;
- use evidence to develop appropriate inferences;
- evaluate use of effective argumentation;
- analyze primary sources (purpose, assumptions, consequences); and
- analyze societal or individual conflicts resulting from the struggle for freedom.

Concept: To understand the theme of freedom and related generalizations, students will be able to:
- support freedom generalizations with evidence from texts;
- apply inductive reasoning to develop generalizations relating to the concepts of freedom, security, individuals, diversity, equality, and democracy;
- describe external and internal threats to personal and national freedom; and
- examine definitions of freedom, means and motives for achieving freedom, and implications for freedom.

 DOI: 10.4324/9781003235217-11

Materials

- Handout 2.5: Concept Organizer
- Handout 8.1: "Special Message to the Congress on Urgent National Needs—Space" by John F. Kennedy
- Handout 8.2: Blank Rhetorical Analysis Wheel
- Handout 8.3: Reasoning About a Situation or Event
- Rubric 1: Product Rubric (Appendix C)

Introductory Activities

Engage students in a quick debate. Ask: *Should the U.S. government fund the NASA Space Program?* Ask students to stand on opposite sides of the room to discuss the issue. Consider asking the following questions during the debate:

- Do you think this amount of money should be spent on space when people in the world are without clean water or food?
- Without the space program, we wouldn't have technologies such as lasers for surgeries, kidney dialysis, or satellite transmissions (or cell phones!). Think of other products that have yet to be developed. Shouldn't it be funded?
- What would the world be like today if we never landed on the moon? Would it be different? What are the consequences of the U.S. being the first to land on the moon?

Text-Dependent Questions

Distribute Handout 8.1: "Special Message to Congress on Urgent National Needs—Space." Explain that this was Section 9 of a speech presented to Congress. Allow students to read the text individually first, or you may allow them to listen to an audio version of the speech (accessible online). Then, read a paragraph at a time aloud, selecting from the following text-dependent questions to lead discussion.

- Kennedy states, "If we are to win the battle between freedom and tyranny that is now going on around the world" to open this section of his speech about space. How does freedom relate to U.S. space achievement? Use textual evidence.
- How does Kennedy use the rhetorical appeal of ethos in the first paragraph? (Sample response: He received advice of the vice president, who is Chairman of the National Space Council, which builds credibility and authority.)
- Based on the first paragraph, what can you infer about the international and political events that elicited his argument?
- According to Kennedy, what is the motivation for space achievement? Is the motivation really just competition?

- What does Kennedy mean by "We go into space because whatever mankind must undertake, free men must fully share"?
- How does Kennedy reason that it will not be just one man going to the moon?
- Of the four goals mentioned, which one do you think would seem the most extreme to Congress at the time?
- Why does Kennedy repeat, "Let it be clear"? What exactly must be clear to the nation?
- According to Kennedy, what responsibilities must Americans take in the space race? Why does he include these as part of his message?
- Kennedy states, "This nation will move forward, with the full speed of freedom, in the exciting adventure of space." What literary technique is he using? What does he mean by "full speed of freedom"? What effect does this have on the audience?
- How does Kennedy inspire vision?

Rhetorical Analysis

Using Handout 8.2: Blank Rhetorical Analysis Wheel, guide students in understanding how the author uses effective argumentation techniques. Consider leading through whole- or small-group discussions, or pairs. Students may take notes on the wheel and draw arrows to illustrate connections between elements. Sample questions and responses to lead analysis include:

- **Context/Purpose:**
  - *What is the historical context?* John F. Kennedy presented this speech May 25, 1961, to Congress. Yuri Gagarin, a Soviet, was the first man to orbit the Earth in space in April 1961; the U.S. fell behind the Soviet Union in the Space Race.
  - *What is Kennedy's purpose?* His goal is to persuade Congress to fund space exploration.

- **Claim:**
  - *What is Kennedy's main claim?* The nation should commit itself to the goals of space exploration.

- **Point of View/Assumptions:**
  - *What is Kennedy's point of view? What are Kennedy's assumptions?* Kennedy believes exploring space will bring advantages to the nation. He believes it will require the nation working together to make the goals a reality.

- **Logos/Technique/Structure:**
  - *How does Kennedy use reasoning to present his points? What techniques are used and how are his points organized?*
    - ◆ **Logos/Reasoning:** He explains the importance of space achievement in the context of current events, requests funding for four national goals, and discusses implications of going to the moon.
    - ◆ **Techniques:** He provides facts about Soviet space achievements, provides clear goals with specific financial detail.
    - ◆ **Structure:** Point by point.

- **Pathos/Technique/Structure:**
  - *How does Kennedy develop emotional appeals?* He evokes a sense of urgency by developing it in context of a battle between tyranny and freedom (contrast), evokes excitement and eagerness toward space achievement through word choice ("holds key to our future," "move forward in the full speed of freedom"), and evokes a sense of responsibility among American people.

- **Ethos/Techniques/Structure:**
  - *How does Kennedy develop credibility and trust?* He mentions advice of the vice president, recognizes the head start of the Soviets, and acknowledges that there is no guarantee the U.S. will win the Space Race.

- **Implications:**
  - *What are the implications/consequences of this document?* It helped to acquire funding that eventually led to landing on the moon.

- **Evaluation:**
  - *How effective is the author in supporting his claim? Is the claim fully supported?* President Kennedy supports the claim of funding space exploration by providing logical reasons, establishing credibility, and evoking excitement for space achievement.

In-Class Activities to Deepen Learning

1. Revisit the quick debate from the introductory activity of this lesson. Ask students: *After hearing this speech, have you changed your mind on your original stance? Why or why not? What is the new space frontier for your generation?*
2. Divide students into two groups: "Reasons why the U.S. government should fund research for human missions to Mars" and "Reasons why the U.S. government should not fund research for human missions to Mars." Students

should read articles related to their side of the issue. (*Note*: This may be assigned as homework to be discussed the next day, or the teacher may pre-select articles to assign.)

3. When students return with their research, have students share their ideas and complete Handout 8.3: Reasoning About a Situation or Event in whole-class discussion. A sample chart is provided in Figure 8.1; student responses may vary. Ask: *Should the U.S. government fund research to prepare human missions to Mars today?*

Concept Connections

1. Ask students to explicitly identify how Kennedy refers to "freedom" in his speech. *How does going to the moon relate to freedom?* Refer to the preamble of the Constitution for students to make connections as to how going to the moon relates to these ideals:

> We the people of the United States, in order to form a more per-fect union, establish justice, insure domestic tranquility, provide for the common defense, promote the general welfare, and secure the blessings of liberty to ourselves and our posterity, do ordain and establish this Constitution for the United States of America.

2. Help students understand how Kennedy's "Special Message to Congress on Urgent National Needs—Space" exemplifies freedom generalizations by leading them through a discussion using Handout 2.5: Concept Organizer. Students should list examples about how the speech demonstrates some of the generalizations. Figure 8.2 provides possible responses; various interpre-tations are encouraged.

Choice-Based Differentiated Products

Students may choose one of the following as individual products to complete (*Note*: Use Rubric 1: Product Rubric in Appendix C to assess student products.):

- Research the number of products that have been developed because of the space program. As you examine the list, create a concept map to show how these can be classified and relate to various disciplines and fields. Determine how these technologies have helped Americans and others experience the ideals outlined in the preamble of the U.S. Constitution (e.g., insure domes-tic tranquility, secure the blessings of liberty, etc.).
- Think about the following question: What does America's moon landing have to do with freedom? Think about the context of the day and the fea-

	NASA	U.S. Government	General Public Yes	General Public No
Point of View				
Assumptions				
Implications				

Figure 8.1. Should the U.S. government fund research to prepare human missions to Mars today? Chart for sample responses.

Freedom requires sacrifice.
In order to take freedom (America) to a new frontier, Congress should fund space goals; the country must commit to the financial cost, resources, and long-term goals.
Freedom requires responsibility.
Kennedy notes, "Whatever mankind must undertake, free men must fully share." Thus, as the U.S. embarks on this endeavor, its responsibility is to share achievements in "world-wide" efforts.
Freedom is threatened by internal and external forces.
The space achievements (which represent freedom ideals, as mentioned in the speech) could be threatened by the choice not to fund the space goals.
Examine the relationship between freedom and another concept (e.g., power, conflict, change, order).
Students may examine relationship between freedom, financial responsibility, the future, frontier, global relations, and other concepts.

Figure 8.2. Sample student responses.

tures of a rhetorical argument. Design an editorial cartoon to argue how America's moon landing impacted freedom.

- Research the Mars One Mission, a nonprofit organization with a goal to have the first human settlement on Mars. After learning more about their specific mission, what would be the short and long-term implications for being a part of their first mission? Evaluate the pros and cons. To what extent would living on Mars redefine freedom? Which freedom generalizations would be most pertinent? Share your reflections with the class.

- Write a letter to the editor discussing your opinion about whether the U.S. should fund NASA as it prepares to send a human to Mars. Consider applying some of the same techniques Kennedy used in his speech and allude to the big idea of freedom.

ELA Practice Tasks

Assign one of following tasks as a performance-based assessment for this lesson:

- Should the U.S. government fund research to prepare for human missions to Mars? In a short research paper, support your claim with relevant evidence from research. Be sure to address counterclaims. Cite resources with appropriate citations.

- How does the organization of Kennedy's ideas help him establish a logical rationale? Explain your answer in an expository essay, citing specific textual evidence from the speech. Be sure to include explanation of logos appeals within the context of overall organization.

Social Studies Content Connections

Refer to the Social Studies Connection Wheel (see Appendix A for information and examples, and Appendix B for a Blank Social Studies Connection Wheel and Social Studies Connections Wheel Guide) to guide students in relating social studies content to the text. The questions below focus on the historical context of the speech. The Big Idea Reflection: Primary Sources (Appendix B) can also be used to relate the text to historical content.

- **Content dependent:** How did technology innovations for space achievement impact at least three other social studies factors (refer to the Social Studies Connection Wheel)?

- **Text dependent:** What were the intended economic, cultural, and political implications of the speech?

	Inference From Evidence
0	Provides no response.
1	Response is limited, vague, and/or inaccurate. There is no justification for answers given.
2	Response is accurate, but lacks adequate explanation. Response includes some justification about the societal conflict.
3	Response is accurate and makes sense. Response includes some justification about the societal conflict.
4	Response is accurate, insightful, interpretive, and well written. Response includes thoughtful justification about the societal conflict.

Figure 8.3. Scoring guidelines for Lesson 8 formative assessment.

Formative Assessment

1. Ask students to respond to the following prompt in a single paragraph: *What can you infer is meant by the quote "But in a very real sense, it will not be one man going to the moon—if we make this judgment affirmatively, it will be an entire nation. For all of us must work to put him there"? How does this quote relate to the societal conflict addressed?*

2. Use the scoring guidelines in Figure 8.3 to evaluate students' assessments.

Handout 8.1

"Special Message to the Congress on Urgent National Needs—Space" *by John F. Kennedy*

Delivered May 25, 1961

Section IX. Space

Finally, if we are to win the battle that is now going on around the world between freedom and tyranny, the dramatic achievements in space which occurred in recent weeks should have made clear to us all, as did the Sputnik in 1957, the impact of this adventure on the minds of men everywhere, who are attempting to make a determination of which road they should take. Since early in my term, our efforts in space have been under review. With the advice of the Vice President, who is Chairman of the National Space Council, we have examined where we are strong and where we are not, where we may succeed and where we may not. Now it is time to take longer strides—time for a great new American enterprise—time for this nation to take a clearly leading role in space achievement, which in many ways may hold the key to our future on earth.

I believe we possess all the resources and talents necessary. But the facts of the matter are that we have never made the national decisions or marshalled the national resources required for such leadership. We have never specified long-range goals on an urgent time schedule, or managed our resources and our time so as to insure their fulfillment.

Recognizing the head start obtained by the Soviets with their large rocket engines, which gives them many months of leadtime, and recognizing the likelihood that they will exploit this lead for some time to come in still more impressive successes, we nevertheless are required to make new efforts on our own. For while we cannot guarantee that we shall one day be first, we can guarantee that any failure to make this effort will make us last. We take an additional risk by making it in full view of the world, but as shown by the feat of astronaut Shepard, this very risk enhances our stature when we are successful. But this is not merely a race. Space is open to us now; and our eagerness to share its meaning is not governed by the efforts of others. We go into space because whatever mankind must undertake, free men must fully share.

I therefore ask the Congress, above and beyond the increases I have earlier requested for space activities, to provide the funds which are needed to meet the following national goals:

First, I believe that this nation should commit itself to achieving the goal, before this decade is out, of landing a man on the moon and returning him safely to the earth. No single space project in this period will be more impressive to mankind, or more important for the long-range exploration of space; and none will be so difficult or expensive to accomplish. We propose to accelerate the development of the appropriate lunar space craft. We propose to develop alternate liquid and solid fuel boosters, much larger than any now being developed, until certain which is superior. We propose additional funds for other engine development and for unmanned explorations—explorations which are particularly important for one purpose which this nation will never overlook: the survival of the man who first makes this daring flight. But in a very real sense, it will not be one man going to the moon—if we make this judgment affirmatively, it will be an entire nation. For all of us must work to put him there.

Secondly, an additional 23 million dollars, together with 7 million dollars already available, will accelerate development of the Rover nuclear rocket. This gives promise of some day providing a means for even more exciting and ambitious exploration of space, perhaps beyond the moon, perhaps to the very end of the solar system itself.

Third, an additional 50 million dollars will make the most of our present leadership, by accelerating the use of space satellites for world-wide communications.

Fourth, an additional 75 million dollars—of which 53 million dollars is for the Weather Bureau—will help give us at the earliest possible time a satellite system for world-wide weather observation.

Let it be clear—and this is a judgment which the Members of the Congress must finally make—let it be clear that I am asking the Congress and the country to accept a firm commitment to a new course of action, a course which will last for many years and carry very heavy costs: 531 million dollars in fiscal '62—an estimated seven to nine billion dollars additional over the next five years. If we are to go only half way, or reduce our sights in the face of difficulty, in my judgment it would be better not to go at all.

Now this is a choice which this country must make, and I am confident that under the leadership of the Space Committees of the Congress, and the Appropriating Committees, that you will consider the matter carefully.

It is a most important decision that we make as a nation. But all of you have lived through the last four years and have seen the significance of space and the adventures in space, and no one can predict with certainty what the ultimate meaning will be of mastery of space.

I believe we should go to the moon. But I think every citizen of this country as well as the Members of the Congress should consider the matter carefully in making their judgment, to which we have given attention over many weeks and months, because it is a heavy burden, and there is no sense in agreeing or desiring that the United States take an affirmative position in outer space, unless we are prepared to do the work and bear the burdens to make it successful. If we are not, we should decide today and this year.

This decision demands a major national commitment of scientific and technical manpower, material and facilities, and the possibility of their diversion from other important activities where they are already thinly spread. It means a degree of dedication, organization and discipline which have not always characterized our research and development efforts. It means we cannot afford undue work stoppages, inflated costs of material or talent, wasteful interagency rivalries, or a high turnover of key personnel.

New objectives and new money cannot solve these problems. They could in fact, aggravate them further—unless every scientist, every engineer, every serviceman, every technician, contractor, and civil servant gives his personal pledge that this nation will move forward, with the full speed of freedom, in the exciting adventure of space.

Name: _____ Date: _____

Handout 8.2
Blank Rhetorical Analysis Wheel

Directions: Draw arrows across elements to show connections.

Text: _____

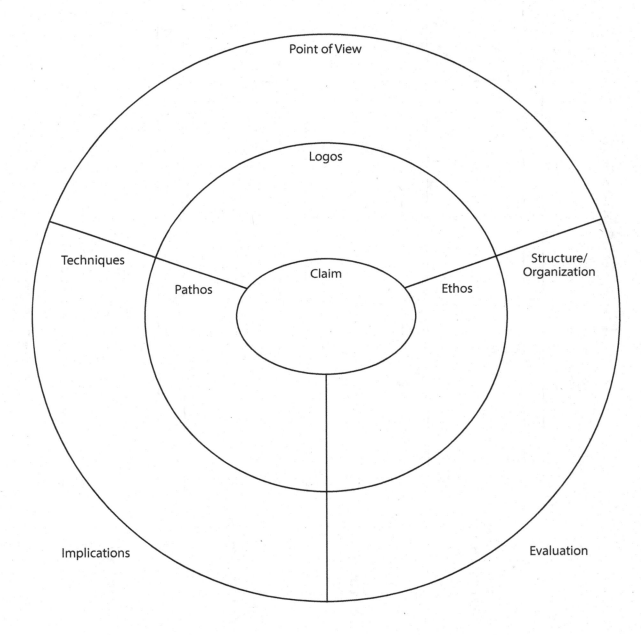

Handout 8.3
Reasoning About a Situation or Event

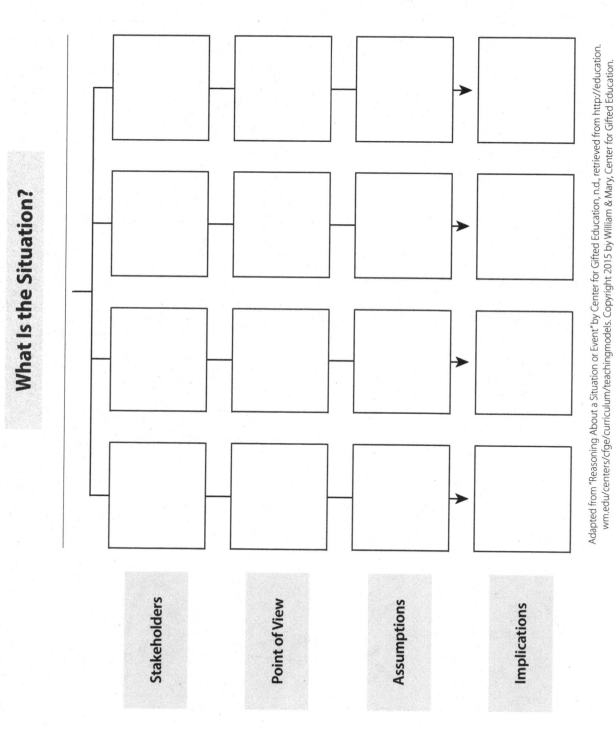

What Is the Situation?

Stakeholders

Point of View

Assumptions

Implications

Adapted from "Reasoning About a Situation or Event" by Center for Gifted Education, n.d., retrieved from http://education. wm.edu/centers/cfge/curriculum/teachingmodels. Copyright 2015 by William & Mary, Center for Gifted Education.

Lesson

9

"We Shall Overcome"
by Lyndon B. Johnson

Goals/Objectives

Content: To analyze and interpret primary source texts, students will be able to:
- explain with evidence how a writer develops and supports a claim,
- respond to interpretations of historical speeches through a variety of contexts,
- compare and contrast various texts and real-world events on themes and generalizations, and
- evaluate rhetorical devices that influence effective argumentation within primary source documents.

Process: To develop thinking, writing, and communication, students will be able to:
- use evidence to develop appropriate inferences;
- evaluate use of effective argumentation;
- analyze primary sources (purpose, assumptions, consequences); and
- analyze societal or individual conflicts resulting from the struggle for freedom.

Concept: To understand the theme of freedom and related generalizations, students will be able to:
- support freedom generalizations with evidence from texts;
- apply inductive reasoning to develop generalizations relating to the concepts of freedom, security, individuals, diversity, equality, and democracy;
- describe external and internal threats to personal and national freedom; and
- examine definitions of freedom, means and motives for achieving freedom, and implications for freedom.

 DOI: 10.4324/9781003235217-12

Materials

- Online access to sample of a Southern literacy test for voting. We suggest the ones available at:
  - http://www.crmvet.org/info/la-test.htm
  - http://www.pbs.org/wnet/jimcrow/literacy_popup.html

- Handout 4.3: Freedom Chart
- Handout 9.1: "We Shall Overcome" by Lyndon B. Johnson
- Handout 9.2: Blank Rhetorical Analysis Wheel
- Rubric 1: Product Rubric (Appendix C)

Introductory Activities

1. Explain to students that Southern states gave literacy tests as part of voting registration starting in the late 1800s through 1965. Even though the 14th and 15th Amendments give citizens the right to vote (regardless of race), these literacy tests and other practices were used to deny African Americans that right. Show students a sample of a literacy test given in the Southern states. Ask students to answer the questions. Explain that prior to 1965, Blacks and other non-Whites in the South were often denied the right to vote if they did not pass these tests. Passing the test was determined by the Registrar, who held no set standards. In some states, Whites were not required to take the literacy tests because they were of "good moral character." Even if African Americans missed only one question, they could still be denied the right to vote.

2. Ask students to conduct initial research on the marches from Selma to Montgomery, AL, in 1965. Students may research the purpose, what happened, and how others responded. You may divide students into groups to explore the First March, Second March, and Third March. Students should share their findings with the class.

Text-Dependent Questions

Distribute Handout 9.1: "We Shall Overcome" by Lyndon B. Johnson. Allow students to read the text individually first, or you may allow them to listen to an audio version of the speech (accessible online). Then, read a paragraph at a time aloud, selecting from the following text-dependent questions to lead discussion.

- What literary technique is Johnson using in the first sentence and what effect does it have on the listener? If you substituted synonyms for the key words, how would the effect be different? What emotions do the key words evoke? (Sample response: He uses alliteration of "d" is used for emphasis and positive connotation.)

- "At times history and fate meet at a single time in a single place to shape a turning point in a man's unending search for freedom." According to Johnson, what are these turning points and why are they turning points? How are these events alike? Why does he refer to the search for freedom as "unending"?

- How does "history and fate" relate to the first sentence of the speech? According to Johnson, what is the "destiny of democracy"? Why does he choose the words "fate" and "destiny" in the introduction? How does this affect his message?

- According to Johnson, how is the issue for equal rights a different challenge than the other challenges faced by the nation?

- Johnson states, "For with a country as with a person, 'What is a man profited, if he shall gain the whole world, and lose his own soul?'" According to this analogy and the context of the text, what is America's "soul"?

- Johnson ends with, "Their cause must be our cause too. Because it is not just Negroes, but really it is all of us, who must overcome the crippling legacy of bigotry and injustice. And we shall overcome." What is significant about the word choice "crippling legacy"? Note the use of pronouns. How does he use pronouns to develop his message? (Sample response: "Their" used with "our" shows a divide; "us" and "we" is a way of uniting all Americans.)

- What is Johnson's tone toward those who disagree with him?

- A promise is a vow that can be kept or broken. When and how does Johnson refer to the "promise" for Americans? Why is this word so important to his message? How does "promise" relate to the ideas of "destiny" and "fate?" (Sample response: He convinces the audience to "keep" the promise and reminds the audience of the journey toward "destiny of democracy.")

- What would Johnson say is the "destiny of democracy"? (Sample response: Freedom for all, including the right to vote for all citizens.)

- How is this speech organized as a narrative about "America's promise"? (Sample response: The speech explains a journey toward fulfilling the promise; Johnson's address tracks the country's progression through references to the "destiny of democracy," the "turning point in history," the "first nation in the history of the world," etc.)

- The phrase "we shall overcome" is directly from song used by African American leaders and protesters as an unofficial anthem for the Civil Rights Movement. Why is it significant that Johnson uses this phrase?

- The speech was originally to be titled "American Promise" but was changed to "We Shall Overcome." Which title best captures the message of the speech? Why?

■ Does Johnson rely on an appeal to morality, the Constitution, or to the American Promise? (Sample response: Johnson assumes issues of the Constitution and morality are resolved; the speech is famous because Johnson makes a transcendent appeal to the heart of America's promise.)

Rhetorical Analysis

Using Handout 9.2: Blank Rhetorical Analysis Wheel, guide students in analyzing how the author uses effective argumentation techniques. Students may take notes on the wheel and draw arrows to illustrate connections between elements. Sample questions and responses to lead analysis include:

■ **Context/Purpose:**
- *What is the historical context?* Johnson presented this speech to Congress on March 15, 1965. One week earlier, police attacked African Americans in Selma, AL, as they prepared to protest unfair voting rights.
- *What is Johnson's purpose?* His goal is to provide justification for a law designed to eliminate illegal barriers to the right to vote.

■ **Claim:**
- *What is Johnson's main claim?* Every American citizen, including "Negroes," must have an equal right to vote.

■ **Point of View/Assumptions:**
- *What are Johnson's assumptions?* Johnson assumes the issue of human rights supersedes issues of states' rights (Southern states would argue that voting issues are matters of state decisions, not the federal government).

■ **Logos/Technique/Structure:**
- *How does Johnson present his points? What techniques are used and how are his points organized?*
   ◆ **Logic/Reasoning:** He introduces that voting rights are an issue of crisis, explains America's purpose, explains how voting rights are denied, explains a bill to eliminate barriers to voting, and concludes with a call to overcome bigotry and injustice.
   ◆ **Techniques:** He uses repetition with parallelism to compare events in Selma to the Revolutionary and Civil Wars ("so it was") and to contrast pride and self-satisfaction with hope and faith ("there is no cause"), and uses the fact that the U.S. was founded on the principle of all men being equal.

♦ **Structure:** He uses short sentence structure at the end to emphasize the simplicity of his rationale. The overall structure is Problem-Solution.

▪ **Pathos/Technique/Structure:**
- *How does Johnson develop emotional appeals?* He uses an inspirational tone in his opening statement ("dignity of man and the destiny of democracy"; alliteration of "d" emphasizes the idea), incites a sense of pride about the government through positive word choice, evokes conviction and moral obligation ("it is wrong, dead wrong"), and inspires a sense of responsibility by inviting all Americans to overcome the "crippling legacy of bigotry and injustice." The word choice of "crippling" implies that America is not what it could be.

▪ **Ethos/Technique/Structure:**
- *How does Johnson develop credibility and trust?* He clearly explains what he is doing as president to ensure rights to vote and refers consistently to the Constitution and great phrases from American history.

▪ **Implications:**
- *What are the implications of this document?* The Voting Rights Act of 1965 was passed.

▪ **Evaluation:**
- *How effective is the author in developing his claim?* Johnson effectively establishes rationale for his claim by using the principles of American history. He establishes the problem by discussing current unfair practices and then introduces the principles of his proposed bill as a solution. He evokes pride about American ideals and responsibility through word choice.

In-Class Activity to Deepen Learning

Johnson alludes to the hymn "We Shall Overcome." Play a video clip of the hymn from YouTube. Ask students to research the background of the hymn or provide background for them (information on the hymn can be easily found through a basic web search). Why was this hymn used in the Civil Rights Movement? How do specific phrases relate to the pursuit of freedom during the Civil Rights Movement, and how do the concepts relate to Johnson's speech?

Concept Connections

Discuss connections to freedom by asking the questions below. The sample answers in Figure 9.1 may be helpful in guiding discussion. Students can record their reflection on Handout 2.5: Concept Organizer, continued from previous lessons. Students may also add to Handout 4.3: Freedom Chart.

- According to Johnson, how is freedom related to responsibility?
- According to Johnson, what is freedom's most significant threat?

Choice-Based Differentiated Products

Students may choose one of the following as independent products to complete (*Note*: Use Rubric 1: Product Rubric in Appendix C to assess student products.):

- Some argue that America was not a democracy until the passage of the Voting Rights Act of 1965. Explore the point of view, assumptions, and implications of various stakeholders. Conduct sufficient research to explore reasons why various historical perspectives would answer "yes" and "no." Pay particular attention to the assumptions of these groups.
- Investigate other ways (besides the literacy test) the South prevented African Americans from voting and allowed illiterate Whites to vote (e.g., "The Grandfather Clause"). Compare and contrast at least three Southern states' approaches. In your opinion, which state was most unfair in its practices? Present your findings to the class.
- Explore how the Voting Rights Act of 1965 affected other groups, such as the Native Americans or non-English speaking groups. Examine how this group has struggled to be represented in democracy. Develop a timeline to show advancements in civil rights for this group and how it may have been inspired by events and ideas related to African American advances in civil rights, Supreme Court cases, or other legislation.

ELA Practice Tasks

Assign one of the following tasks as a performance-based assessment for this lesson:

- In an explanatory essay, compare and contrast the arguments for women's suffrage used by Carrie Chapman Catt to the arguments for equal voting rights used by Lyndon B. Johnson. How are their techniques similar? How are they different? Cite relevant examples from both texts in your essay.
- How does Johnson use ideas of "America's promise" to persuade his audience? Respond in an essay relating the concept to his message, claim, support, and rhetorical appeals. Cite relevant examples from the text.

Freedom requires sacrifice.
Because Americans in history have fought and died for freedom's sake, we should not dishonor them in denying non-Whites the right to vote. Denying this right would be dishonoring the idea for which they died.
Freedom requires responsibility.
As "Americans," we all have a responsibility to fulfill the promises given in the Constitution—the equal right to "choose your own leaders."
Freedom is threatened by internal and external forces.
Freedom is threatened for non-Whites in the denial to vote through unfair practices. The force is internal, which is central to Johnson's argument.
Examine the relationship between freedom and another concept (e.g., power, conflict, change, order).
Although freedom was promised, its fulfillment was thwarted by authority (states). The destiny for democracy is freedom for all.

Figure 9.1. Sample student responses.

Social Studies Content Connections

Refer to the Social Studies Connection Wheel (see Appendix A for information and examples, and Appendix B for a Blank Social Studies Connection Wheel and Social Studies Connections Wheel Guide) to guide students in relating social studies content to the text. The Big Idea Reflection: Primary Sources (Appendix B) can also be used to relate the text to historical content.

- **Content dependent:** How does social equity interact with two other factors from the Social Studies Connections Wheel to produce the problem addressed in the speech?
- **Text dependent:** Why did Johnson link the events in Lexington, Concord, and Appomattox with those in Selma? Why was this important to the introduction of the speech?
- **Text dependent:** What was Johnson's intended outcome for America upon the conclusion of his speech? How do you know? (Cite textual evidence.)
- **Content dependent:** What was significant about the location of Selma, AL? How did this location's culture impact the events of Selma?

Formative Assessment

1. Ask students to respond to the following prompt in a single paragraph: *What does this speech reveal about the big idea of freedom? Be sure to include a freedom generalization in your response.*
2. Use the scoring guidelines in Figure 9.2 to evaluate students' assessments.

	Concept/Theme
0	Provides no response.
1	Response is limited, vague, and/or inaccurate.
2	Response lacks adequate explanation. Response does not relate or create a generalization about freedom. Little or no evidence from text.
3	Response is accurate and makes sense. Response relates to or creates an idea about freedom with some relation to the text.
4	Response is accurate, insightful, and well written. Response relates to or creates a generalization about freedom with evidence from the text.

Figure 9.2. Scoring guidelines for Lesson 9 formative assessment.

Handout 9.1

"We Shall Overcome" *by Lyndon B. Johnson*

Delivered March 15, 1965

Mr. Speaker, Mr. President, Members of the Congress:

I speak tonight for the dignity of man and the destiny of democracy. I urge every member of both parties, Americans of all religions and of all colors, from every section of this country, to join me in that cause.

At times history and fate meet at a single time in a single place to shape a turning point in man's unending search for freedom. So it was at Lexington and Concord. So it was a century ago at Appomattox. So it was last week in Selma, Alabama. There, long-suffering men and women peacefully protested the denial of their rights as Americans. Many were brutally assaulted. One good man, a man of God, was killed.

There is no cause for pride in what has happened in Selma. There is no cause for self-satisfaction in the long denial of equal rights of millions of Americans. But there is cause for hope and for faith in our democracy in what is happening here tonight. For the cries of pain and the hymns and protests of oppressed people have summoned into convocation all the majesty of this great government—the government of the greatest nation on earth. Our mission is at once the oldest and the most basic of this country: to right wrong, to do justice, to serve man.

In our time we have come to live with the moments of great crisis. Our lives have been marked with debate about great issues—issues of war and peace, issues of prosperity and depression. But rarely in any time does an issue lay bare the secret heart of America itself. Rarely are we met with a challenge, not to our growth or abundance, or our welfare or our security, but rather to the values, and the purposes, and the meaning of our beloved nation.

The issue of equal rights for American Negroes is such an issue.

And should we defeat every enemy, and should we double our wealth and conquer the stars, and still be unequal to this issue, then we will have failed as a people and as a nation. For with a country as with a person, "What is a man profited, if he shall gain the whole world, and lose his own soul?"

There is no Negro problem. There is no Southern problem. There is no Northern problem. There is only an American problem. And we are met here tonight as Americans—not as Democrats or Republicans. We are met here as Americans to solve that problem.

This was the first nation in the history of the world to be founded with a purpose. The great phrases of that purpose still sound in every American heart, North and South: "All men are created equal," "government by consent of the governed," "give me liberty or give me death." Well, those are not just clever words, or those are not just empty theories. In their name Americans have fought and died for two centuries, and tonight around the world they stand there as guardians of our liberty, risking their lives.

Those words are a promise to every citizen that he shall share in the dignity of man. This dignity cannot be found in a man's possessions; it cannot be found in his power, or in his position. It really rests on his right to be treated as a man equal in opportunity to all others. It says that he shall share in freedom, he shall choose his leaders, educate his children, provide for his family according to his ability and his merits as a human being. To apply any other test—to deny a man his hopes because of his color, or race, or his religion, or the place of his birth is not only to do injustice, it is to deny America and to dishonor the dead who gave their lives for American freedom.

Our fathers believed that if this noble view of the rights of man was to flourish, it must be rooted in democracy. The most basic right of all was the right to choose your own leaders. The history of this country, in large measure, is the history of the expansion of that right to all of our people. Many of the issues of civil rights are very complex and most difficult. But about this there can and should be no argument.

Every American citizen must have an equal right to vote.

There is no reason which can excuse the denial of that right. There is no duty which weighs more heavily on us than the duty we have to ensure that right.

Yet the harsh fact is that in many places in this country men and women are kept from voting simply because they are Negroes. Every device of which human ingenuity is capable has been used to deny this right. The Negro citizen may go to register only to be told that the day is wrong, or the hour is late, or the official in charge is absent. And if he persists, and if he manages to present himself to the registrar, he may be disqualified because he did not spell out his middle name or because he abbreviated a word on the application. And if he manages to fill out an application, he is given a test. The registrar is the sole judge of whether he passes this test. He may be asked to recite the entire Constitution, or explain the most complex provisions of State law. And even a college degree cannot be used to prove that he can read and write.

For the fact is that the only way to pass these barriers is to show a white skin. Experience has clearly shown that the existing process of law cannot overcome systematic and ingenious discrimination. No law that we now have on the books—and I have helped to put three of them there—can ensure the right to vote when local officials are determined to deny it. In such a case our duty must be clear to all of us. The Constitution says that no person shall be kept from voting because of his race or his color. We have all sworn an oath before God to support and to defend that Constitution. We must now act in obedience to that oath.

Wednesday, I will send to Congress a law designed to eliminate illegal barriers to the right to vote.

The broad principles of that bill will be in the hands of the Democratic and Republican leaders tomorrow. After they have reviewed it, it will come here formally as a bill. I am grateful for this opportunity to come here tonight at the invitation of the leadership to reason with my friends, to give them my views, and to visit with my former colleagues. I've had prepared a more comprehensive analysis of the legislation which I had intended to transmit to the clerk tomorrow, but which I will submit to the clerks tonight. But I want to really discuss with you now, briefly, the main proposals of this legislation.

Handout 9.1, Continued

This bill will strike down restrictions to voting in all elections—Federal, State, and local—which have been used to deny Negroes the right to vote. This bill will establish a simple, uniform standard which cannot be used, however ingenious the effort, to flout our Constitution. It will provide for citizens to be registered by officials of the United States Government, if the State officials refuse to register them. It will eliminate tedious, unnecessary lawsuits which delay the right to vote. Finally, this legislation will ensure that properly registered individuals are not prohibited from voting.

I will welcome the suggestions from all of the Members of Congress—I have no doubt that I will get some—on ways and means to strengthen this law and to make it effective. But experience has plainly shown that this is the only path to carry out the command of the Constitution.

To those who seek to avoid action by their National Government in their own communities, who want to and who seek to maintain purely local control over elections, the answer is simple: open your polling places to all your people.

Allow men and women to register and vote whatever the color of their skin.

Extend the rights of citizenship to every citizen of this land.

There is no constitutional issue here. The command of the Constitution is plain. There is no moral issue. It is wrong—deadly wrong—to deny any of your fellow Americans the right to vote in this country. There is no issue of States' rights or national rights. There is only the struggle for human rights. I have not the slightest doubt what will be your answer . . .

But even if we pass this bill, the battle will not be over. What happened in Selma is part of a far larger movement which reaches into every section and State of America. It is the effort of American Negroes to secure for themselves the full blessings of American life. Their cause must be our cause too. Because it's not just Negroes, but really it's all of us, who must overcome the crippling legacy of bigotry and injustice.

And we shall overcome.

Name: _____   Date: _____

Handout 9.2
Blank Rhetorical Analysis Wheel

Directions: Draw arrows across elements to show connections.

Text: _____

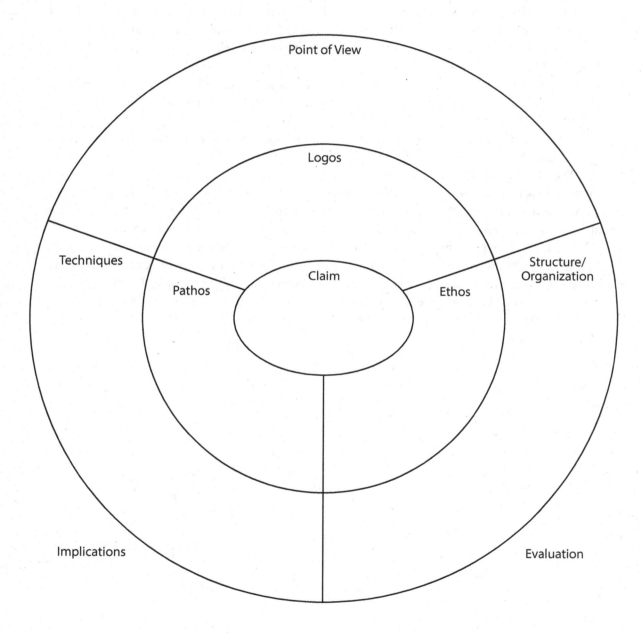

Purpose/Context

Point of View

Logos

Techniques

Pathos

Claim

Ethos

Structure/
Organization

Implications

Evaluation

Created by Emily Mofield, Ed.D., & Tamra Stambaugh, Ph.D., 2015.

Lesson

"9/11 Address to the Nation"
by George W. Bush

Goals/Objectives

Content: To analyze and interpret primary source texts, students will be able to:
- explain with evidence how a writer develops and supports a claim,
- respond to interpretations of historical speeches through a variety of contexts,
- compare and contrast various texts and real-world events on themes and generalizations, and
- evaluate rhetorical devices that influence effective argumentation within primary source documents.

Process: To develop thinking, writing, and communication, students will be able to:
- use evidence to develop appropriate inferences;
- evaluate use of effective argumentation;
- analyze primary sources (purpose, assumptions, consequences); and
- analyze societal or individual conflicts resulting from the struggle for freedom.

Concept: To understand the theme of freedom and related generalizations, students will be able to:
- support freedom generalizations with evidence from texts;
- apply inductive reasoning to develop generalizations relating to the concepts of freedom, security, individuals, diversity, equality, and democracy;
- describe external and internal threats to personal and national freedom; and
- examine definitions of freedom, means and motives for achieving freedom, and implications for freedom.

Materials

- Student copies of "Nothing Gold Can Stay" by Robert Frost

145

DOI: 10.4324/9781003235217-13

- Student copies of poem "If They Can Speak" by Rosanne Pellicane
- Handout 4.3: Freedom Chart
- Handout 10.1: "9/11 Address to the Nation" by George W. Bush
- Handout 10.2: Blank Rhetorical Analysis Wheel
- Rubric 1: Product Rubric (Appendix C)

Introductory Activities

1. Ask students to read the poem, "Nothing Gold Can Stay" by Robert Frost. Then, lead students through a line-by-line close reading. Ask the following questions:
   - What is meant by "her hardest hue to hold"?
   - Is this poem about endings or beginnings? Does this poem exemplify the idea that "change is good" or "change is bad"?
   - Does each change show a shift to good or a shift to something bad?
   - What meaning does the allusion to The Fall (in Genesis) play in the poem? (Help students understand the concept of *felix culpa*—blessed fall. Without the fall of man, there would have been no need of reconciliation to God or redemption. In essence, without the bad, the good cannot be appreciated. Without evil, can there be good?)
   - Note that "Dawn goes down to day" does not say "dawn goes down *today*." Given that the sun goes *up* at dawn as it reaches day, why did Frost say dawn goes "down" to day?
   - How does the line "dawn goes down to day" relate to the idea of *felix culpa*? (*Note*: It appears though each change shows a diminishing of value, each change actually leads to something better [green to gold, leaf to a flower, leaf to leaf]. Thus, "Eden sank to grief" actually leads to something better. Eden sinking to grief leads to a need for redemption ["blessed fall"] and appreciation of "good." Loss is balanced by gain.)

2. Read "If They Could Speak" by Rosanne Pellicane, and lead a class discussion with the following questions:
   - How does "If They Could Speak" relate to "Nothing Gold Can Stay"? Cite specific lines and phrases from "Nothing Gold Can Stay" and explain how they relate to ideas in Pellicane's poem.
   - What message do both poems portray?

3. Show a short video clip of some of the September 11th events (as you see appropriate for your classroom).

Text-Dependent Questions

Distribute Handout 10.1: "9/11 Address to the Nation" by George W. Bush. Allow students to read the text individually first, or you may allow them to listen to an audio version of the speech (accessible online). Then, read a paragraph at a time aloud, selecting from the following text-dependent questions to lead discussion.

- Why does Bush specifically name the types of people that were victims?
- Why is it important that he mentions the imagery of the attack: "The pictures of the airplanes flying into buildings . . . "? What rhetorical appeal is he using and what is its effect?
- What analogies and metaphors does Bush use to develop his argument? (Sample response: Foundation of buildings compared to foundation of America, steel of American resolve, America as a beacon of light.)
- What is important about the word choice "resolve"? When and where does he repeat this word? What effect does he intend to give the audience?
- What parts of the speech use an ethos appeal to build Bush's credibility and trust in the nation? (Sample response: "I implemented our government response plans . . . ")
- What major contrasts does Bush use in his speech and what effect do they have on the message? How do these contrasts relate to ideas in "Nothing Gold Can Stay"? (Sample response: Worst of human nature/best of America.)
- How does the biblical allusion contribute to the message of the speech?
- How would you describe George W. Bush's style and what impact does this have on the audience? (Sample response: Short sentence structure, easy to understand; the world was in a panic and needed clarity.)
- What four words from the speech best capture the essence of Bush's message? Can you put these words together in a sentence to explain his message? (Sample response: Strong, freedom, terrorist, fear, etc.)
- What logic does Bush use to support his claim that Americans will win the war against terrorism? (Sample response: "We've stood down enemies before, and we will do so this time," etc.)
- What phrases and ideas show the idea of *felix culpa* (i.e., good coming from bad)? What connections can you make with this speech and the previously read poems? (Can good exist without evil? Can heroism exist without the tragedy?)

148 *Rhetorical Analysis*

Using Handout 10.2: Blank Rhetorical Analysis Wheel, guide students in analyzing how the author uses effective argumentation techniques. Students may take notes on the wheel and draw arrows to illustrate connections between elements. Sample questions and responses to lead analysis include:

- **Context/Purpose:**
  - *What is the historical context?* Bush presented this speech on the evening of September 11, 2001, through a television broadcast following the terrorist attacks.
  - *What is Bush's purpose?* His goal is to respond to the terrorist attacks of 9/11 and to encourage the American people to go forward in defending freedom.

- **Claim:**
  - *What is Bush's main claim?* Although the U.S. has been attacked, the American people are resolved to stay strong.

- **Point of View/Assumptions:**
  - *What is Bush's point of view? What assumptions does he make?* As president, Bush is speaking from a point of view of protecting and defending the nation. He makes an assumption in making no distinction between terrorists and those who harbor them.

- **Logos/Technique/Structure:**
  - *How does Bush use reasoning to present his points? What techniques are used, and how does he organize his points?*
    - ◆ **Logos/Reasoning:** He explains how terrorist attacks affected citizens' lives, explains why America is strong, explains policy points, and concludes to move forward and defend freedom.
    - ◆ **Techniques:** He uses imagery as he gives facts of the attacks (e.g., pictures of the planes) and draws the rationale that America has previously stood down enemies and will do so again.
    - ◆ **Structure:** He presents the problem and states a solution through policy points.

- **Pathos/Technique/Structure:**
  - *How does Bush develop emotional appeals? Where are these placed and why?* He includes specific people as victims to build an emotional connection, uses negative word connotations when speaking of the enemy, evokes feelings of pride and patriotism through positive word choice, and ends with an allusion to Psalm 23 to provide feelings of comfort.

- **Ethos/Technique/Structure:**
  - *How does Bush develop credibility and trust?* He explains how he implemented the government emergency response, introduces policy points, and uses pronouns "we" and "us" to build a connection with the audience.

- **Implications:**
  - *What are the implications/consequences of this speech?* The War on Terror results.

- **Evaluation:**
  - *How effective is the author in supporting his or her claim?* Bush uses a balance of appeals to support the claim that although America has been attacked, the American people are resolved to stay strong. He could perhaps include more facts and evidence about the attacks, but he provides adequate facts about policy points. He uses extensive use of pathos appeals to evoke emotions.

In-Class Activity to Deepen Learning

Have students work in groups to develop a visual to show how two of the three texts relate to the idea of "good coming from bad." This may be a chart, concept map, or diagram. Include specific words and phrases from all three texts to show connections. A sample chart with responses is provided in Figure 10.1.

Concept Connections

1. Discuss connections to freedom by asking the following questions:
   - According to Bush, how is responsibility related to freedom?
   - What generalization can be made about resolve and freedom?

2. Have students add their notes to Handout 4.3: Freedom Chart. As an additional option, students may add to Handout 2.5: Concept Organizer. Figure 10.2 provides some sample responses.

Choice-Based Differentiated Products

Students may choose one of the following as independent products to complete (*Note*: Use Rubric 1: Product Rubric in Appendix C to assess student products.):
   - Write your own memorial poem about the event, a person, a group of people, or a place associated with September 11th. Include the idea of "good

Nothing Gold Can Stay	Comparison	George W. Bush's Speech
"her hardest hue to hold"	Something of great value (e.g., freedom) is being threatened.	"Our very freedom came under attack." "Thousands of lives were suddenly ended."
"So Eden sank to grief"	Evil entered the world, but provided a need for "good."	"Terrorists can shake the foundations of our biggest buildings . . ." Heroes come out of tragedies.
"Dawn goes down to day"	Though the goodness ends, loss is balanced by gain . . . the day moves forward.	"No one will keep this light from shining . . . "

Figure 10.1. Sample comparison chart.

Freedom requires sacrifice.
American citizens must unite in resolve for justice and peace, accept the war on terror, and defend freedom.
Freedom requires responsibility.
In order to defend freedom, America will fight a war against terrorism. Intelligence and law enforcement are taking responsibility in finding those who committed the evil acts.
Freedom is threatened by internal and external forces.
Freedom is threatened by the external forces of terrorism.
Examine the relationship between freedom and another concept (e.g., power, conflict, change, order).
Students may consider connections between freedom, resolve, justice, peace, war, and other concepts.

Figure 10.2. Sample student responses.

coming from bad" as it relates uniquely to your specific chosen topic. Include at least 10 phrases from the texts and underline them within your poem.

- Compare Bush's speech to Roosevelt's speech given after the attack on Pearl Harbor or to Madison's proclamation given after the burning of the capitol in the War of 1812. Create a chart to show at least four similar techniques used and evaluate which speech is most effective in its message about pre-serving and defending freedom.

- Choose phrases from Bush's speech that relate to elements of freedom discussed in this unit so far. Create a collage using at least six quotes from this speech, images associated with September 11th, as well as symbols associated with freedom.
- Take at least 12 phrases from any of the texts read in this lesson (poems and speech). Arrange them into an artistic work of art (designed to depict an image associated with September 11th). The art should illustrate an idea related to defending freedom or heroes rising in the midst of tragedy.

ELA Practice Tasks

Assign one of the following tasks as a performance-based assessment for this lesson:

- Explain how "Nothing Gold Can Stay" by Robert Frost and George W. Bush's speech "9/11 Address to the Nation" both illustrate the idea of *good coming from bad*. Cite specific phrases and quotes from the texts to support your explanations.
- How does Bush evoke emotional appeals within his speech and how does it contribute to his central idea? In an explanatory essay, provide textual evidence to support your claim.

Social Studies Content Connections

Refer to the Social Studies Connection Wheel (see Appendix A for information and examples, and Appendix B for a Blank Social Studies Connection Wheel and Social Studies Connections Wheel Guide) to guide students in relating social studies content to the text. The questions below focus on the historical context of the speech. The Big Idea Reflection: Primary Sources (Appendix B) can also be used to relate the text to historical content.

- **Text dependent:** How are the concepts of power and conflict addressed within Bush's speech? Explain the cause-effect relationships between these two concepts.
- **Content dependent:** Would the content of the speech be the same if the attacks happened in a different U.S. location? To Americans traveling abroad? Use what you know about past historical events as well as factors from the Social Studies Connections Wheel to explain your answer.

Claim and Evidence	
0	Provides no response.
1	Response is limited, vague, and/or inaccurate. Only the claim is mentioned with little support.
2	Response is accurate and makes sense. Response relates to or creates an idea about freedom with some relation to the text.
3	Response is accurate and makes sense. Response includes one to two examples of support for the claim.
4	Response is accurate, insightful, and well written. Response includes two to three examples of support for the claim with textual evidence.

Figure 10.3. Scoring guidelines for Lesson 10 formative assessment.

Formative Assessment

1. Ask students to respond to the following prompt in a single paragraph: *What is Bush's main claim and how is it supported?*
2. Use the scoring guidelines in Figure 10.3 to evaluate students' assessments.

Handout 10.1

"9/11 Address to the Nation" *by George W. Bush*

Delivered September 11, 2001

Good evening.

Today, our fellow citizens, our way of life, our very freedom came under attack in a series of deliberate and deadly terrorist acts.

The victims were in airplanes or in their offices—secretaries, businessmen and women, military and federal workers. Moms and dads. Friends and neighbors.

Thousands of lives were suddenly ended by evil, despicable acts of terror.

The pictures of airplanes flying into buildings, fires burning, huge structures collapsing, have filled us with disbelief, terrible sadness and a quiet, unyielding anger.

These acts of mass murder were intended to frighten our nation into chaos and retreat. But they have failed. Our country is strong. A great people has been moved to defend a great nation.

Terrorist attacks can shake the foundations of our biggest buildings, but they cannot touch the foundation of America. These acts shatter steel, but they cannot dent the steel of American resolve.

America was targeted for attack because we're the brightest beacon for freedom and opportunity in the world. And no one will keep that light from shining.

Today, our nation saw evil, the very worst of human nature, and we responded with the best of America, with the daring of our rescue workers, with the caring for strangers and neighbors who came to give blood and help in any way they could.

Immediately following the first attack, I implemented our government's emergency response plans. Our military is powerful, and it's prepared. Our emergency teams are working in New York City and Washington, D.C., to help with local rescue efforts.

Our first priority is to get help to those who have been injured and to take every precaution to protect our citizens at home and around the world from further attacks.

The functions of our government continue without interruption. Federal agencies in Washington which had to be evacuated today are reopening for essential personnel tonight and will be open for business tomorrow.

Our financial institutions remain strong, and the American economy will be open for business as well.

The search is underway for those who are behind these evil acts. I've directed the full resources for our intelligence and law enforcement communities to find those responsible and bring them to justice. We will make no distinction between the terrorists who committed these acts and those who harbor them.

I appreciate so very much the members of Congress who have joined me in strongly condemning these attacks. And on behalf of the American people, I thank the many world leaders who have called to offer their condolences and assistance.

America and our friends and allies join with all those who want peace and security in the world and we stand together to win the war against terrorism.

Tonight I ask for your prayers for all those who grieve, for the children whose worlds have been shattered, for all whose sense of safety and security has been threatened. And I pray they will be comforted by a power greater than any of us spoken through the ages in Psalm 23: "Even though I walk through the valley of the shadow of death, I fear no evil, for You are with me."

This is a day when all Americans from every walk of life unite in our resolve for justice and peace. America has stood down enemies before, and we will do so this time.

None of us will ever forget this day, yet we go forward to defend freedom and all that is good and just in our world.

Thank you. Good night and God bless America.

Name: _____ Date: _____

Handout 10.2
Blank Rhetorical Analysis Wheel

Directions: Draw arrows across elements to show connections.

Text: _____

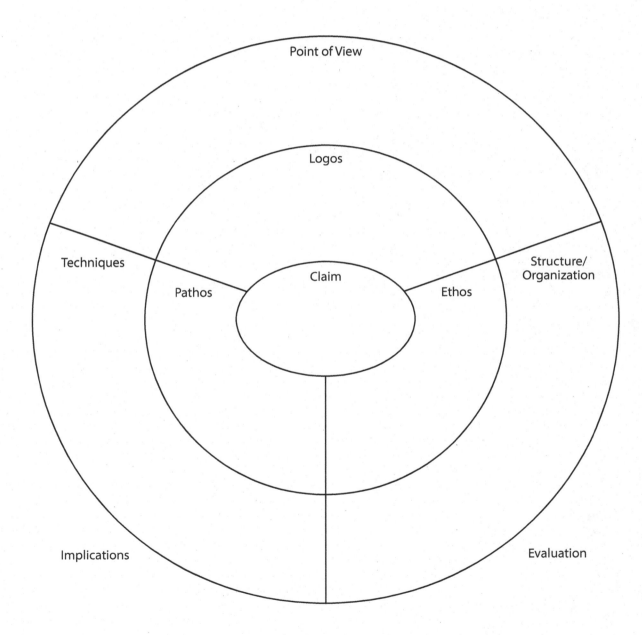

Purpose/Context

Point of View

Logos

Techniques

Structure/
Organization

Pathos

Claim

Ethos

Implications

Evaluation

Created by Emily Mofield, Ed.D., & Tamra Stambaugh, Ph.D., 2015.

Lesson

11

"First Inaugural Address"
by Barack Obama

Goals/Objectives

Content: To analyze and interpret primary source texts, students will be able to:
- explain with evidence how a writer develops and supports a claim,
- respond to interpretations of historical speeches through a variety of contexts,
- compare and contrast various texts and real-world events on themes and generalizations, and
- evaluate rhetorical devices that influence effective argumentation within primary source documents.

Process: To develop thinking, writing, and communication, students will be able to:
- use evidence to develop appropriate inferences;
- evaluate use of effective argumentation;
- analyze primary sources (purpose, assumptions, consequences); and
- analyze societal or individual conflicts resulting from the struggle for freedom.

Concept: To understand the theme of freedom and related generalizations, students will be able to:
- support freedom generalizations with evidence from texts;
- apply inductive reasoning to develop generalizations relating to the concepts of freedom, security, individuals, diversity, equality, and democracy;
- describe external and internal threats to personal and national freedom; and
- examine definitions of freedom, means and motives for achieving freedom, and implications for freedom.

DOI: 10.4324/9781003235217-14

Materials

- (Optional) Student copies of President Lincoln's "First Inaugural Address" (from Lesson 5)
- Handout 11.1: "Gettysburg Address" by Abraham Lincoln
- Handout 11.2: Excerpts From "First Inaugural Address" by Barack Obama
- Handout 11.3: Blank Rhetorical Analysis Wheel
- Rubric 1: Product Rubric (Appendix C)

Introductory Activities

1. Connect President Barack Obama's First Inaugural Address to Lincoln's Gettysburg Address. Obama's speech alludes to Lincoln's speech and commemorates the 200th anniversary of Lincoln's birth. Obama's inaugural activities involved taking the same train route Abraham Lincoln had made to Washington, DC, for his First Inaugural Address in 1861. As students participate in this lesson, help students make connections between Lincoln's texts (e.g., First Inaugural Address, studied in Lesson 5, and "The Gettysburg Address") and Obama's First Inaugural Address.

2. Ask students to read Handout 11.1: "The Gettysburg Address" by Abraham Lincoln. This short close reading of "The Gettysburg Address" will provide insight as students read Obama's First Inaugural Address. Ask students:
   - What is Lincoln's main claim?
   - What is the main contrast in the speech (e.g., birth vs. death)? How is this established? Examine each time he employs this contrast and how it affects the message.
   - What are the three most important words in this text?
   - How does the first sentence relate to the last phrase of the text: "This nation, under God, shall have a new birth of freedom—and that the government for the people, by the people, for the people, shall not perish from the earth"?
   - What does Lincoln mean by "new birth of freedom"? Why is it "new"?
   - How would you structure a four-part outline of this address? (Responses should include: acknowledgement of Founding Father ideals, acknowledgement of struggle/testing of these ideals, acknowledgement of sacrifice, the living generation will be devoted to freedom.)

Text-Dependent Questions

Distribute Handout 11.2: Excerpts From "First Inaugural Address" by Barack Obama. Allow students to read the text individually first. Then, read a paragraph at a time aloud, selecting from the following text-dependent questions to lead discussion. Although the text is an excerpt, the teacher may wish to show students the entire speech via video.

- The first paragraph uses several words and phrases to describe American ideals. What are these words, specifically, and what emotions do they evoke? What does he mean by "better history"?
- How does Obama inspire listeners to appreciate the past?
- Obama mentions, "For they have forgotten what this country has already done; what free men and women can achieve when imagination is joined to common purpose." What can we infer is this "common purpose"?
- What does Obama mean by " . . . our power grows from its prudent use; our security emanates from the justness of our cause, the force of our example, the tempering qualities of humility and restraint," and what is its purpose in the larger context of the speech?
- How does Obama support the claim that America's patchwork heritage is a strength?
- What is Obama asking of the American people?
- According to Obama, what is the "meaning of our liberty and creed"?
- What is meant by the metaphor, "let us brave once more the icy currents . . . "? How does it support Obama's main claim?
- What four words from the text best capture Obama's message?
- Is Obama's speech primarily epideictic (i.e., addressing present, praising good/blaming bad) or deliberative (i.e., presenting policy for future)?
- How is the phrase " . . . why a man whose father less than 60 years ago might not have been served at a local restaurant can now stand before you to take a most sacred oath . . . " an appeal to both pathos and ethos?
- How does Obama relate Lincoln's idea of "new freedom" in the context of this speech"? (Sample response: America has new challenges and new responsibilities.)
- Which phrase or sentence from the speech best relates to America "finding freedom"?

Rhetorical Analysis

Using Handout 11.3: Blank Rhetorical Analysis Wheel, guide students in analyzing how the writer uses effective argumentation techniques. Students may take notes on the wheel and draw arrows to illustrate connections between elements. Sample questions and responses to lead analysis include:

- **Context/Purpose:**
  - *What is the historical context?* Obama delivered this speech as his First Inaugural Address on January 20, 2009.

- *What is Obama's purpose?* His goal is to explain that America will continue to carry freedom, even through difficult times.

- Claim:
  - *What is Obama's main claim?* In the face of hardships, Americans have a duty to shape America's future with its timeless ideals.

- **Point of View/Assumptions:**
  - *What is Obama's point of view? What assumptions does he make?* He acknowledges that there will be many hardships ahead during his term. He explains an inclusive cultural point of view. He makes an assumption that peace is attainable for corrupt leaders (if they are willing to unclench their fists).

- **Logos/Technique/Structure:**
  - *How does Obama use reasoning to present his points? How are the points developed and how are they organized?*
    - **Logos/Reasoning:** He addresses the same points made by Lincoln in the Gettysburg Address: Founding Father ideals, testing of these ideals, acknowledgement of sacrifice, the living generation is devoted to freedom.
    - **Techniques:** He gives examples of how America earned its greatness, acknowledges and addresses opposing viewpoint, uses metaphor of a patchwork heritage to describe cultural unity, and includes quotes from history.
    - **Structure:** Inductive. Obama provides evidence to build his conclusion that is given at the end of the speech: "Let us brave once more the icy currents and endure what storms might come. "

- **Pathos/Technique/Structure:**
  - *How does Obama develop emotional appeals?* He evokes a sense of determination by discussing work ethic of past generations through word choice (e.g., "hands were raw," "dust ourselves off"), evokes feelings of pride and patriotism through positive word choice throughout the speech, and refers to scripture and God to evoke a sense of reverence for the ideas of freedom.

- **Ethos/Technique/Structure:**
  - *How does Obama develop credibility and trust?* He makes references to the Founding Fathers, refers to himself as a son of a father who may have been denied service in a restaurant 60 years prior—personally connects with hardships of America's past.

▪ **Implications:**
  • *What are the implications of this speech?* This speech is remembered for its call to defend old truths in the face of new challenges. It is of historical importance because Barack Obama was the first elected African American president.

▪ **Evaluation:**
  • *How effective is the author in supporting his or her claim?* To support his claim, Obama includes several examples of the challenges that have been experienced in America's past and acknowledges the challenges ahead. He evokes hope and determination that America will endure as a great nation through new challenges. He builds credibility by basing his points on principles of history.

In-Class Activities to Deepen Learning

1. Ask: *How is Obama's speech structurally similar to Lincoln's Gettysburg Address? Use specific examples.* Guide students to understanding the similar pattern in "The Gettysburg Address." Refer back to the pattern established in "The Gettysburg Address":
   ▪ acknowledgement of Founding Father ideals,
   ▪ acknowledgement of struggle/testing of these ideals,
   ▪ acknowledgement of sacrifice, and
   ▪ the living generation will be devoted to freedom.

2. Ask students to note how Obama's speech has a similar pattern. Students should refer to specific textual evidence.
3. Remind students that Obama's First Inaugural Address events revolved around a "New Birth of Freedom" tour. Ask: *What is the significance and relationship of the tour as it symbolically relates to Obama's inauguration?*
4. Assign the following roles for a fishbowl discussion. Students in the inner circle will discuss answers to questions from the point of view of the assigned individual. Observers can take notes and ask additional questions during the discussion. Fishbowl inner circle participants may rotate out halfway during the discussion so that outside participants may participate.
   ▪ Patrick Henry
   ▪ President James Madison
   ▪ President Andrew Jackson
   ▪ Frederick Douglass
   ▪ President Abraham Lincoln
   ▪ Carrie Chapman Catt

- President Franklin D. Roosevelt
- President John F. Kennedy
- President Lyndon B. Johnson
- President George W. Bush
- President Barack Obama

5. Students should speak in first person from the point of view of their role. When appropriate, students should use textual evidence to support their point of view on the following issues:
    - What kind of freedom did you promote (or deny)?
    - How are your thoughts about freedom similar or different from the others in this room?
    - What are your points of disagreement?
    - In what ways did you see the threat to freedom similar to others in the room?
    - Do you feel that the message you conveyed to America was fully embraced?
    - What are the implications of your speech and how are they realized today?

Concept Connections

Guide students in understanding how Obama's "First Inaugural Address" exemplifies freedom generalizations by leading students in a discussion using Handout 2.5: Concept Organizer. Students should list examples about how the speech demonstrates some of the generalizations. Provide guidance as needed. Figure 11.1 provides possible responses, although various interpretations are encouraged.

Choice-Based Differentiated Products

Students may choose one of the following as independent products to complete (*Note*: Use Rubric 1: Product Rubric in Appendix C to assess student products.):
- Research more about Barack Obama's "New Birth of Freedom" tour as part of the Inaugural Celebration. Explain the significance and relationship of the tour as it symbolically relates to Obama's inauguration. Present your ideas in an essay, a multimedia presentation, or a brochure. Be sure to make connections between Lincoln, Obama, and the "new birth of freedom."
- Compare Obama's "First Inaugural Address" to Lincoln's "First Inaugural Address" (refer to Lesson 5). Examine similarities and differences between Lincoln's and Obama's approaches, techniques, structure, and historical situations. Create a Venn diagram or a comparison chart.

Freedom requires sacrifice.
Obama remarks on the previous sacrifices in American history to preserve freedom.
Freedom requires responsibility.
Obama is asking that Americans take on the difficult task of facing current challenges, upholding the old truths that promote freedom.
Freedom is threatened by internal and external forces.
Obama briefly mentions external corrupt power; we might infer this as a threat. Freedom is threatened internally when we forget the enduring truths of our past within perilous times; we must work hard in difficult times.
Examine the relationship between freedom and another concept (e.g., power, conflict, change, order).
Even through change and difficult times, freedom will endure.

Figure 11.1. Sample student responses.

- Using specific words and phrases (at least 10) from Obama's speech, develop an original poem about freedom.
- Write an editorial in response to Obama's speech. Provide your opinion on whether or not the ideas in the speech were fulfilled during his presidency. Cite specific evidence from the speech in your editorial.
- Read Obama's "Second Inaugural Address." How does it compare and contrast to his "First Inaugural Address"? Do you notice any changes in mood or tone? What similar literary and rhetorical techniques does he use? Explain your comparisons and contrasts in a chart or essay, citing evidence from the text.

ELA Practice Tasks

Assign one of the following tasks as a performance-based assessment for this lesson.

- How do ideas in Obama's "First Inaugural Address" relate to Lincoln's "Gettysburg Address"? Write a well-developed essay that explains the connections between the two texts.
- Has America achieved Lincoln's "new birth of freedom"? How would Obama answer this question? In an argumentative essay, use textual evidence from Obama's "First Inaugural Address" to support your stance.

Claim and Evidence	
0	Provides no response.
1	Response is limited, vague, and/or inaccurate. Only the claim is mentioned with little support.
2	Response lacks adequate explanation. Some parts of the response are correct, but the response only vaguely addresses the author's claim and evidence. Response lacks support.
3	Response is accurate and makes sense. Response includes one to two examples of support for the claim.
4	Response is accurate, insightful, and well written. Response includes two to three examples of support for the claim with textual evidence.

Figure 11.2. Scoring guidelines for Lesson 11 formative assessment.

Social Studies Content Connections

Refer to the Social Studies Connection Wheel (see Appendix A for information and examples, and Appendix B for a Blank Social Studies Connection Wheel and Social Studies Connections Wheel Guide) to guide students in relating social studies content to the text. The Big Idea Reflection: Primary Sources (Appendix B) can also be used to relate the text to historical content.

- **Text dependent:** How are the concepts of power, culture, and world context addressed in President Obama's speech? How are these connected to each other and to his main message?
- **Content dependent:** What were President Obama's intended outcomes for America? Refer to at least three social studies factors in your answer and explain how they relate. In your opinion, were his outcomes realized? Explain with evidence.

Formative Assessment

1. Ask students to respond to the following prompt in a single paragraph: *What is President Obama's main claim and how is it supported?*
2. Use the scoring guidelines in Figure 11.2 to evaluate students' assessments.

Handout 11.1

"Gettysburg Address" *by Abraham Lincoln*

Delivered November 19, 1863

Four score and seven years ago our fathers brought forth on this continent, a new nation, conceived in Liberty, and dedicated to the proposition that all men are created equal.

Now we are engaged in a great civil war, testing whether that nation, or any nation so conceived and so dedicated, can long endure. We are met on a great battle-field of that war. We have come to dedicate a portion of that field, as a final resting place for those who here gave their lives that that nation might live. It is altogether fitting and proper that we should do this.

But, in a larger sense, we can not dedicate—we can not consecrate—we can not hallow—this ground. The brave men, living and dead, who struggled here, have consecrated it, far above our poor power to add or detract. The world will little note, nor long remember what we say here, but it can never forget what they did here. It is for us the living, rather, to be dedicated here to the unfinished work which they who fought here have thus far so nobly advanced. It is rather for us to be here dedicated to the great task remaining before us—that from these honored dead we take increased devotion to that cause for which they gave the last full measure of devotion—that we here highly resolve that these dead shall not have died in vain—that this nation, under God, shall have a new birth of freedom—and that government of the people, by the people, for the people, shall not perish from the earth.

Name: _____ Date: _____

Handout 11.2

Excerpts From "First Inaugural Address" *by Barack Obama*

Delivered January 21, 2009

My fellow citizens: I stand here today humbled by the task before us, grateful for the trust you've bestowed, mindful of the sacrifices borne by our ancestors . . .

We remain a young nation. But in the words of Scripture, the time has come to set aside childish things. The time has come to reaffirm our enduring spirit; to choose our better history; to carry forward that precious gift, that noble idea passed on from generation to generation: the God-given promise that all are equal, all are free, and all deserve a chance to pursue their full measure of happiness.

In reaffirming the greatness of our nation we understand that greatness is never a given. It must be earned. Our journey has never been one of short-cuts or settling for less. It has not been the path for the faint-hearted, for those that prefer leisure over work, or seek only the pleasures of riches and fame. Rather, it has been the risk-takers, the doers, the makers of things—some celebrated, but more often men and women obscure in their labor—who have carried us up the long rugged path towards prosperity and freedom.

For us, they packed up their few worldly possessions and traveled across oceans in search of a new life. For us, they toiled in sweatshops, and settled the West, endured the lash of the whip, and plowed the hard earth.

For us, they fought and died in places like Concord and Gettysburg, Normandy and Khe Sahn.

Time and again these men and women struggled and sacrificed and worked till their hands were raw so that we might live a better life. They saw America as bigger than the sum of our individual ambitions, greater than all the differences of birth or wealth or faction.

This is the journey we continue today. We remain the most prosperous, powerful nation on Earth. Our workers are no less productive than when this crisis began. Our minds are no less inventive, our goods and services no less needed than they were last week, or last month, or last year. Our capacity remains undiminished. But our time of standing pat, of protecting narrow interests and putting off unpleasant decisions—that time has surely passed. Starting today, we must pick ourselves up, dust ourselves off, and begin again the work of remaking America . . .

Now, there are some who question the scale of our ambitions, who suggest that our system cannot tolerate too many big plans. Their memories are short, for they have forgotten what this country has already done, what free men and women can achieve when imagination is joined to common purpose, and necessity to courage.

As for our common defense, we reject as false the choice between our safety and our ideals. Our Founding Fathers—(applause)—our Founding Fathers, faced with perils that we can scarcely imagine, drafted a charter to assure the rule of law and the rights of man—a charter expanded by the blood of generations. Those ideals still light the world, and we will not give them up for expedience sake.

And so, to all the other peoples and governments who are watching today, from the grandest capitals to the small village where my father was born, know that America is a friend of each nation, and every man, woman and child who seeks a future of peace and dignity. And we are ready to lead once more.

Recall that earlier generations faced down fascism and communism not just with missiles and tanks, but with the sturdy alliances and enduring convictions. They understood that our power alone cannot protect us, nor does it entitle us to do as we please. Instead they knew that our power grows through its prudent use; our security emanates from the justness of our cause, the force of our example, the tempering qualities of humility and restraint.

We are the keepers of this legacy. Guided by these principles once more we can meet those new threats that demand even greater effort, even greater cooperation and understanding between nations. We will begin to responsibly leave Iraq to its people and forge a hard-earned peace in Afghanistan. With old friends and former foes, we'll work tirelessly to lessen the nuclear threat, and roll back the specter of a warming planet. We will not apologize for our way of life, nor will we waver in its defense. And for those who seek to advance their aims by inducing terror and slaughtering innocents, we say to you now that our spirit is stronger and cannot be broken—you cannot outlast us, and we will defeat you.

For we know that our patchwork heritage is a strength, not a weakness. We are a nation of Christians and Muslims, Jews and Hindus, and non-believers. We are shaped by every language and culture, drawn from every end of this Earth; and because we have tasted the bitter swill of civil war and segregation, and emerged from that dark chapter stronger and more united, we cannot help but believe that the old hatreds shall someday pass; that the lines of tribe shall soon dissolve; that as the world grows smaller, our common humanity shall reveal itself; and that America must play its role in ushering in a new era of peace.

To the Muslim world, we seek a new way forward, based on mutual interest and mutual respect. To those leaders around the globe who seek to sow conflict, or blame their society's ills on the West, know that your people will judge you on what you can build, not what you destroy. To those who cling to power through corruption and deceit and the silencing of dissent, know that you are on the wrong side of history, but that we will extend a hand if you are willing to unclench your fist . . .

Our challenges may be new. The instruments with which we meet them may be new. But those values upon which our success depends—honesty and hard work, courage and fair play, tolerance and curiosity, loyalty and patriotism—these things are old. These things are true. They have been the quiet force of progress throughout our history.

What is demanded, then, is a return to these truths. What is required of us now is a new era of responsibility—a recognition on the part of every American that we have duties to ourselves, our nation and the world; duties that we do not grudgingly accept, but rather seize gladly, firm in the knowledge that there is nothing so satisfying to the spirit, so defining of our character than giving our all to a difficult task.

Handout 11.2, Continued

This is the price and the promise of citizenship. This is the source of our confidence—the knowledge that God calls on us to shape an uncertain destiny. This is the meaning of our liberty and our creed, why men and women and children of every race and every faith can join in celebration across this magnificent mall; and why a man whose father less than 60 years ago might not have been served in a local restaurant can now stand before you to take a most sacred oath.

So let us mark this day with remembrance of who we are and how far we have traveled. In the year of America's birth, in the coldest of months, a small band of patriots huddled by dying campfires on the shores of an icy river. The capital was abandoned. The enemy was advancing. The snow was stained with blood. At the moment when the outcome of our revolution was most in doubt, the father of our nation ordered these words to be read to the people:

"Let it be told to the future world . . . that in the depth of winter, when nothing but hope and virtue could survive . . . that the city and the country, alarmed at one common danger, came forth to meet [it]."

America: In the face of our common dangers, in this winter of our hardship, let us remember these timeless words. With hope and virtue, let us brave once more the icy currents, and endure what storms may come. Let it be said by our children's children that when we were tested we refused to let this journey end, that we did not turn back nor did we falter; and with eyes fixed on the horizon and God's grace upon us, we carried forth that great gift of freedom and delivered it safely to future generations.

Thank you. God bless you. And God bless the United States of America.

Name: _____ Date: _____

Handout 11.3
Blank Rhetorical Analysis Wheel

Directions: Draw arrows across elements to show connections.

Text: _____

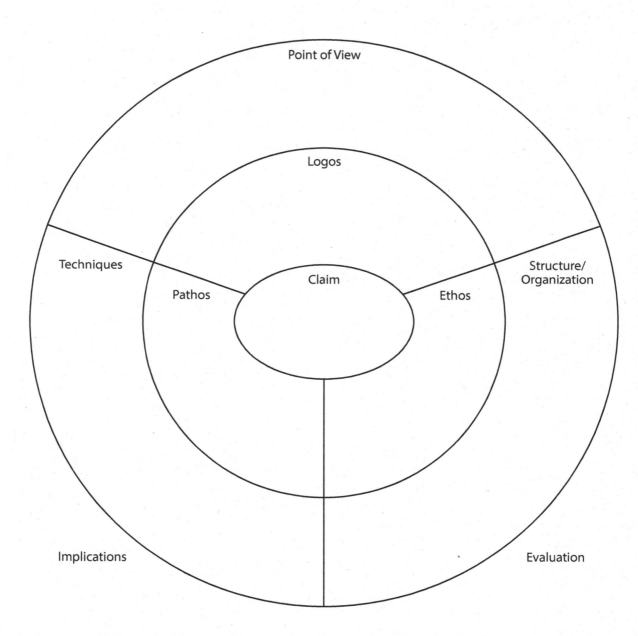

Lesson

12

Final Reflection and Culminating Project

Goals/Objectives

Content: To analyze and interpret primary source texts, students will be able to:
- explain with evidence how a writer develops and supports a claim,
- respond to interpretations of historical speeches through a variety of contexts,
- compare and contrast various texts and real-world events on themes and generalizations, and
- evaluate rhetorical devices that influence effective argumentation within primary source documents.

Process: To develop thinking, writing, and communication, students will be able to:
- reason through an issue by analyzing points of view, assumptions, and implications;
- use evidence to develop appropriate inferences;
- evaluate use of effective argumentation;
- analyze primary sources (purpose, assumptions, consequences); and
- analyze societal or individual conflicts resulting from the struggle for freedom.

Concept: To understand the theme of freedom and related generalizations, students will be able to:
- support freedom generalizations with evidence from texts;
- apply inductive reasoning to develop generalizations relating to the concepts of freedom, security, individuals, diversity, equality, and democracy;
- describe external and internal threats to personal and national freedom; and
- examine definitions of freedom, means and motives for achieving freedom, and implications for freedom.

 DOI: 10.4324/9781003235217-15

Materials

- Students may need copies of Blank Rhetorical Analysis Wheel, Reasoning About a Situation or Event, and/or Handout 2.5: Concept Organizer, depending on the project they choose. See Appendix B for models.
- Handout 12.1: *Finding Freedom* Culminating Project
- Rubric 2: Culminating Project Rubric (Appendix C)

Discussion

1. Remind students about the concepts explored in this unit:
   - Freedom requires sacrifice.
   - Freedom requires responsibility.
   - Freedom is threatened by internal and external sources.

2. Students should review their responses to the concept organizers (Handout 2.5: Concept Organizer and Handout 4.3: Freedom Chart) from previous lessons. Ask: *What patterns do you notice? Do you see any similarities? What are the major contrasts? What additional generalizations about freedom might be made based on this unit? What evidence is there to support those generalizations?*

Student Reflection

Assign Student Reflections on Handout 12.1: Culminating Project (you may choose to assign all of them or part of them).

Choice-Based Differentiated Products

1. Assign Culminating Project (see Handout 12.1). At teacher discretion, students can present parts of their projects to the class.
2. Use Rubric 2: Culminating Project Rubric (Appendix C) to assess student products.

Culminating ELA Practice Task

Assign the following task as a performance-based assessment for this lesson: *How has the concept of freedom changed over the course of American history? After reading the documents in this unit, write an essay that explores this issue. Refer to at least four sources from the unit and cite specific textual evidence from these sources in your essay.*

Handout 12.1
Finding Freedom Culminating Project

STUDENT REFLECTION

1. Create a concept map about freedom based on the ideas presented within this unit. Develop your map with major ideas, individuals, and events that shape your thinking about freedom.
2. In a one- to two-page reflection, describe how this unit has impacted your learning. How does this unit relate to you personally? How have you deepened your understanding of freedom?

CULMINATING PROJECT

Choose one activity to demonstrate your understanding of the content, processes, and concepts presented in this unit:

1. Develop your own speech that addresses a contemporary controversy on freedom. You may be flexible in your definition for freedom. Consider contemporary topics such as Internet privacy policies, equality education for gifted learners, freedom of religion, freedom of speech, the line between security and freedom in airports, etc. Develop your speech with effective rhetorical appeals and techniques. Complete the Rhetorical Analysis Wheel and Concept Organizer on your own speech. Deliver your speech to the class.
2. Choose one specific speech or document from this unit. Find at least three additional primary sources that relate to it (e.g., Carrie Chapman Catt—read three other speeches about women's suffrage from the same time period; Patrick Henry—read three other documents relating to inciting the American Revolution, etc.). The documents may be from multiple perspectives. Explain in a few paragraphs how the documents allude to ideas of freedom, citing evidence from the texts. Complete a Rhetorical Analysis Wheel on each document.
3. Using Reasoning About a Situation or Event, develop your own question about a current issue (relating to a freedom idea). Examine at least two stakeholder viewpoints on the issue. Complete Reasoning About a Situation or Event. Then, create a visual collage or multimedia movie to answer the question "How is freedom threatened today?" Incorporate abstract symbols, words, pictures, and quotes about freedom, power, conflict, change, or other related concepts. Also turn in a written description of symbols used.

4. What is America's journey in finding freedom? Answer this question in a short movie production. Reread at least four of the speeches or documents studied within the unit. Find the most significant or compelling sections (quotes, words, phrases) from these documents. Then develop a short movie (2–4 minutes) using Windows MovieMaker (or other software) with music, images, and voice narration using text phrases as well as your own reflections. The purpose and message of your movie must relate to freedom (e.g., What is freedom? Who is freedom for?). Use your completed Finding Freedom Chart for organizing your thoughts.

5. Has America found freedom? Evaluate a contemporary issue such as the government's threats on personal privacy, gun control, controversies on freedom of speech, etc. Apply Reasoning About a Situation or Event to the issue. In addition, write an argumentative essay that addresses the question "Has America found freedom?" as it relates to your selected issue. Use at least five credible sources to support your claim. Relate at least two freedom generalizations within your essay.

ELA PRACTICE TASK

How has the concept of freedom changed over the course of American history? After reading the documents in this unit, write an essay that explores this issue. Refer to at least four sources from the unit and cite specific textual evidence from these sources in your essay.

Name: _____ Date: _____

Posttest

"Third Inaugural Address" by *Franklin D. Roosevelt*

Directions: Please read the passage and answer the questions thoroughly and thoughtfully. Be sure to provide evidence to support your answer. After reading, complete the questions within 30 minutes.

Delivered January 20, 1941

On each national day of Inauguration since 1789, the people have renewed their sense of dedication to the United States.

In Washington's day the task of the people was to create and weld together a Nation.

In Lincoln's day the task of the people was to preserve that Nation from disruption from within.

In this day the task of the people is to save that Nation and its institutions from disruption from without.

To us there has come a time, in the midst of swift happenings, to pause for a moment and take stock—to recall what our place in history has been, and to rediscover what we are and what we may be. If we do not, we risk the real peril of isolation, the real peril of inaction.

Lives of Nations are determined not by the count of years, but by the lifetime of the human spirit. The life of a man is threescore years and ten: a little more, a little less. The life of a Nation is the fullness of the measure of its will to live.

There are men who doubt this. There are men who believe that democracy, as a form of government and a frame of life, is limited or measured by a kind of mystical and artificial fate that, for some unexplained reason, tyranny and slavery have become the surging wave of the future—and that freedom is an ebbing tide.

But we Americans know that this is not true.

Eight years ago, when the life of this Republic seemed frozen by a fatalistic terror, we proved that this is not true. We were in the midst of shock—but we acted. We acted quickly, boldly, decisively.

These later years have been living years—fruitful years for the people of this democracy. For they have brought to us greater security and, I hope, a better understanding that life's ideals are to be measured in other than material things.

Most vital to our present and to our future is this experience of a democracy which successfully survived crisis at home; put away many evil things; built new structures on enduring lines; and, through it all, maintained the fact of its democracy.

For action has been taken within the three-way framework of the Constitution of the United States. The coordinate branches of the Government continue freely to function. The Bill of Rights remains inviolate. The freedom of elections is wholly maintained. Prophets of the downfall of American democracy have seen their dire predictions come to naught.

No, democracy is not dying.

Posttest, Continued

We know it because we have seen it revive—and grow.

We know it cannot die—because it is built on the unhampered initiative of individual men and women joined together in a common enterprise—an enterprise undertaken and carried through by the free expression of a free majority.

We know it because democracy alone, of all forms of government, enlists the full force of men's enlightened will.

We know it because democracy alone has constructed an unlimited civilization capable of infinite progress in the improvement of human life.

We know it because, if we look below the surface, we sense it still spreading on every continent—for it is the most humane, the most advanced, and in the end the most unconquerable of all forms of human society.

A Nation, like a person, has a body—a body that must be fed and clothed and housed, invigorated and rested, in a manner that measures up to the standards of our time.

A Nation, like a person, has a mind—a mind that must be kept informed and alert, that must know itself, that understands the hopes and the needs of its neighbors—all the other Nations that live within the narrowing circle of the world.

A Nation, like a person, has something deeper, something more permanent, something larger than the sum of all its parts. It is that something which matters most to its future—which calls forth the most sacred guarding of its present.

It is a thing for which we find it difficult—even impossible to hit upon a single, simple word.

And yet, we all understand what it is—the spirit—the faith of America. It is the product of centuries. It was born in the multitudes of those who came from many lands—some of high degree, but mostly plain people—who sought here, early and late, to find freedom more freely . . .

Its vitality was written into our own Mayflower Compact, into the Declaration of Independence, into the Constitution of the United States, into the Gettysburg Address.

Those who first came here to carry out the longings of their spirit, and the millions who followed, and the stock that sprang from them—all have moved forward constantly and consistently toward an ideal which in itself has gained stature and clarity with each generation . . . .

In the face of great perils never before encountered, our strong purpose is to protect and to perpetuate the integrity of democracy.

For this we muster the spirit of America, and the faith of America.

We do not retreat. We are not content to stand still. As Americans, we go forward, in the service of our country, by the will of God.

Name: _____ Date: _____

QUESTIONS

1. What is Roosevelt's main claim and how is it supported? Provide textual evidence.

2. How effective is Roosevelt in developing his argument? Support your answer by referring to elements of effective argumentation.

3. What can you infer is meant by the phrase "There are men who believe . . . that freedom is an ebbing tide" and how does it relate to the conflict addressed?

4. What does this passage reveal about the big idea of freedom? Support your answer with textual evidence.

Name: _____ Date: _____

Postest Rubric

"Third Inaugural Address" by *Franklin D. Roosevelt*

	0	1	2	3	4
Question 1: Content: Claim and Evidence	Provides no response.	Response is limited, vague, and/or inaccurate. Only the claim is mentioned with little support.	Response lacks adequate explanation. Some parts of the response are correct, but the response only vaguely addresses the author's claim and evidence. Response lacks support.	Response is accurate and makes sense. Response includes one to two examples of support for the claim.	Response is accurate, insightful, and well written. Response includes two to three examples of support for the claim with textual evidence.
Question 2: Content: Effective Rhetoric	Provides no response.	Response is limited and vague. Response only partially answers the question. A rhetorical element is not mentioned or is merely named with no example from text.	Response is accurate with one to two rhetorical elements mentioned. Response includes limited or no evidence from text.	Response is appropriate and accurate, describing at least two rhetorical elements to support effective argumentation. Response includes some evidence from the text.	Response is insightful and well supported, describing at least three rhetorical elements. Response includes substantial evidence from the text.
Question 3: Inference From Evidence	Provides no response.	Response is limited, vague, and/or inaccurate. There is no justification for answers given.	Response is accurate, but lacks adequate explanation. Response includes some justification about the societal conflict.	Response is accurate and makes sense. Response includes some justification about the societal conflict.	Response is accurate, insightful, interpretive, and well written. Response includes thoughtful justification about the societal conflict.
Question 4: Concept/ Theme	Provides no response.	Response is limited, vague, and/or inaccurate.	Response lacks adequate explanation. Response does not relate or create a generalization about freedom. Little or no evidence from text.	Response is accurate and makes sense. Response relates to or creates an idea about freedom with some relation to the text.	Response is accurate, insightful, and well written. Response relates to or creates a generalization about freedom with evidence from the text.

References

Assouline, S., Colangelo, N., VanTassel-Baska, J., & Lupkowski-Shoplik, A. (2015). (Eds). *A nation empowered: Evidence trumps the excuses holding back America's brightest students.* Iowa City: University of Iowa, The Connie Belin & Jacqueline N. Blank International Center for Gifted Education and Talent Development.

Colangelo, N., Assouline, S., & Gross, M. U. M. (2004). *A nation deceived: How schools hold back America's brightest students* (V.II.). Iowa City: University of Iowa, The Connie Belin & Jacqueline N. Blank International Center for Gifted Education and Talent Development.

Kulik, J. A., & Kulik, C. L. C. (1992). Meta-analytic findings on grouping programs. *Gifted Child Quarterly, 36,* 73–77.

Reid, R. F. (1997). New England rhetoric and the French War. 1754–1760: A case study in the rhetoric of war. *Communication Monographs, 43,* 259–285.

Rogers, K. B. (2007). Lessons learned about educating the gifted and talented: A synthesis of the research on educational practice. *Gifted Child Quarterly, 51,* 382–396.

Steenbergen-Hu, S., & Moon, S. M. (2010). The effects of acceleration on high-ability learners: A meta-analysis. *Gifted Child Quarterly, 55,* 39–53.

VanTassel-Baska, J. (1986). Effective curriculum and instruction models for talented students. *Gifted Child Quarterly, 30,* 164–169.

VanTassel-Baska, J., & Stambaugh, T. (2008). *What works: 20 years of curriculum research and development for high-ability learners.* Center for Gifted Education, College of William and Mary. Waco, TX: Prufrock Press.

Appendix A
Instructions for Using the Models

RHETORICAL ANALYSIS WHEEL INSTRUCTIONS

The Rhetorical Analysis Model is used to analyze how an author develops and supports an argument. Students examine how a writer achieves his or her purpose by analyzing how several elements work together to create an effective argument. This includes thinking about the rhetorical situation (e.g., purpose, context, audience), means of persuasion (e.g., ethos, logos, and pathos appeals), and rhetorical strategies (e.g., techniques, evidence, structure, etc.). The author develops a claim through the use of three rhetorical appeals: logos (reasoning), pathos (emotion), and ethos (credibility) in response to the situation. These rhetorical appeals are developed by point of view, specific strategies, techniques, and organization. The model allows students to see connections between multiple elements (e.g., credibility is influenced by point of view, specific techniques are used to evoke emotion, structure develops strong logos appeals, etc.).

Overview of Aristotle's Rhetorical Appeals

Aristotle's rhetoric includes logos, ethos, and pathos appeals. This enhances a writer's ability to persuade an audience.

- **Logos:** How the author establishes good reasoning to make his message make sense. This includes major points, use of evidence, syllogisms, examples, evidence, facts, statistics, etc. Text focused.
- **Pathos:** How the author appeals to the audience's emotion. Audience focused.
- **Ethos:** How the author develops credibility and trust. Author focused.

Using the Rhetorical Analysis Wheel

The Rhetorical Analysis Wheel can be used to analyze how an author develops a claim through rhetorical appeals, techniques, and structure. Students also think through the point of view, assumptions, purpose, and implications of the document. It is meant to be interactive. The inner circle conceptually spins so that it interacts with elements on the outer circle.

The Rhetorical Analysis Wheel Guide (Appendix B) shows specific prompts to guide students in thinking through each separate element. The teacher may simply refer to the model during instruction, or students may take notes on the Blank Rhetorical Analysis Wheel using arrows to show how elements relate. It is suggested that students first note the answers to each element separately on the graphic organizer, and then discuss how they influence each other. Consider making a poster of the Rhetorical Analysis Wheel Guide to refer to throughout the unit. Students can make their own interactive paper-plate model of the wheel. Two different colored papers may be used for the inner and outer circles, secured with a brass paper fastener. Students may use the wheels as visuals in small groups.

Some teachers of younger grades may wish to focus on how the author supports a central idea by using relevant and sufficient evidence. A simpler version of the Rhetorical Analysis may be used. See Appendix B for the Text Analysis Wheel. The Text Analysis Wheel does not focus on the rhetorical appeals (logos, ethos, and pathos) to support a claim; rather, it focuses on why the author chose to use specific points to advance a central idea.

Sample questions for rhetorical analysis. The following questions can be asked for analyzing argument. Note that complexity is added by combining elements.

- **Purpose:**
  - *What is the author's purpose?*

- **Context/Audience:**
  - *Who is the audience and what is the historical situation?*
  - *What is the main problem in the historical context?*

- **Claim:**
  - *What is the main claim or message of the text?*

- **Techniques:**
  - *What specific techniques does the writer use to develop his or her claim?* Here are some examples of specific techniques that may be asked:
    - **Language:** Consider how specific word choice and style develops tone.
    - **Positive and negative connotations of words:** Consider how words evoke feelings.
    - **Personification:** Human qualities given to nonhuman objects/ideas.

- ◆ **Simile:** A figure of speech that compares two unlike things using "like" or "as."
- ◆ **Metaphor:** A direct comparison between two unlike things.
- ◆ **Hyperbole:** An extreme exaggeration.
- ◆ **Allusion:** A reference to a historical or biblical work, person, or event. The writer assumes the reader can make connections between the allusion and text being read.
- ◆ **Imagery:** Formation of mental images that appeal to the senses.
- ◆ **Parallelism:** Using similar grammatical structures in order to emphasize related ideas.
- ◆ **Repetition:** Repeating the same wording for emphasis, clarity, or emotional impact.
- ◆ **Contrast:** A striking difference of ideas.
- ◆ **Rhetorical question:** A question asked by the writer, but is not expected to be answered aloud. It evokes reflection.
- ◆ **Liberty rhetoric:** Using patriotic appeals for freedom.
- ◆ **War rhetoric:** Reasoning to convince war is necessary.
- ◆ **Syllogism:** A form of deductive logic—a conclusion drawn from two premises. Example: If x=y, y=z, then x=z. If citizens can vote and if women are citizens, then women should be allowed to vote.
- ◆ **Use of evidence, facts, statistics, examples, and counterclaims (strongly connects with logos):** Explicit support for the argument.

■ **Point of View/Assumptions:**
- *What is the writer's point of view toward the topic?*
- *What assumptions does the writer make?*
- *What is the writer's unstated premise or belief? What does the writer take for granted about the audience?*

■ **Structure/Organization:**
- *How does the writer organize ideas (e.g., problem-solution, point by point, chronologically, sequentially, compare/contrast)?*
- *Where is the thesis? Why is it here?*
- *Does the writer structure his message deductively or inductively?*

■ **Logos (Focus on Text)**
- *What reasoning is used to help the argument make sense? What are the main points?*
- *Are statements easy to accept or does the writer need to provide more evidence?*

- *What research, facts, statistics, or expert opinions are used? Are these sufficient?*
  - Logos/Structure: *How does the structure of the document help the writer's argument make sense?*
  - Logos/Point of View: *Does the writer assume that the audience already accepts a premise? What do the writer's examples and facts (or lack of) reveal about his or her assumptions about the audience?*
  - Logos/Techniques: *Which techniques are used to help the writer logically form his or her argument (e.g., syllogisms, comparisons, parallelisms, use of statistics, examples, etc.)?*
  - Logos /Context: *How do the problem, context, and audience influence the writer's approach in developing a logical argument? Since the historical situation is what it is, how does this influence the way the writer organizes his reasoning?*

- **Pathos (Focus on Audience)**
  - *How does the writer appeal to the audience's emotions (guilt, fear, pride, etc.)?*
  - *What word connotations or imagery does the writer use to evoke emotion in the audience?*
  - *How do pathos appeals help the writer establish his or her claim?*
    - Pathos/Point of View: *How does the writer's tone and point of view impact the desired emotional response? How does the writer's bias influence the desired emotional response?*
    - Pathos/Technique: *What techniques does the writer use to evoke emotion among the audience (e.g., repetition, liberty rhetoric, war rhetoric, similes, hyperbole, symbolism, rhetorical questions)?*
    - Pathos/Structure: *Where does the writer place the emotional appeals? Why is this important? Do pathos appeals change throughout the text? How? Why? How does this enhance or take away from the argument?*
    - Pathos/Context: *How does the historical situation/problem influence how the writer uses pathos appeals? How do pathos appeals help the writer accomplish his or her desired effect?*

- **Ethos (Focus on Writer)**
  - *Is the writer credible?*
  - *How does the writer establish trust?*
  - *Are sources credible?*
  - *Does the writer respect an opposing viewpoint?*
  - *Does the writer address counterclaims? How?*

- *How does ethos help the writer establish an effective argument?*
  - Ethos/Technique: *What techniques does the writer use to establish credibility (e.g., uses reliable sources, discusses character/reputation, etc.)?*
  - Ethos/Point of View: *Does the writer's bias take away from his or her credibility? Do the writer's assumptions about the opposing point of view reduce his or her credibility?*
  - Ethos/Structure: *Where in the document does the writer develop his or her credibility? Why is it significant he or she places his or her ethos appeals here? Where does the writer address counterclaims? How does he or she address the counterclaim, and how does this enhance or reduce his or her credibility?*
  - Ethos/Context: *Why is it important for the writer to develop trust with this audience in this historical situation? What must the writer consider about the audience when establishing his or her credibility?*

- **Implications:**
  - *What are the short- and long-term consequences of this document?*

- **Evaluation:**
  - *How effective is the writer in developing his or her claim? To what extent is the purpose fulfilled?*
  - *Is there a balance of pathos, ethos, and logos appeals?*
  - *Is there too much bias or emotional manipulation? Is there adequate evidence to support the claim(s)? Is the evidence credible, rational, and organized logically?*

Students should consider the author's purpose (to entertain, inform, persuade, express) when determining how effective the argument is. For example, it may not be necessary to provide counterarguments if the purpose of the text is not to persuade. Students should also consider the balance of logos, ethos, and pathos appeals.

Example Rhetorical Analysis Lesson

Students should read the excerpt from Franklin D. Roosevelt's Second Inaugural Address. This is the text used for the pretest.

Step 1: Text-dependent questions for close reading. Lead students through a close reading of the text for initial comprehension. You may also ask students to paraphrase sections of the text into their own words.

- According to President Roosevelt, what brings an ever richer life to Americans?

- Why does Roosevelt personify Comfort, Opportunism, and Timidity? How are these "voices" considered distractions?
- What are some of the positive aspects of the current state of affairs?
- According to the text, why is prosperity dangerous?
- What is meant by "prosperity already tests the persistence of our progressive purpose"?
- Which one of Roosevelt's "I see" statements is most powerful?
- According to the text, how do we test our progress?
- What is Roosevelt's solution to the problems of tens of millions?
- What four words are most important to the text? Can you put these four words together in a sentence to summarize FDR's main message?

Step 2: Teach elements of rhetorical analysis. Teach students some basic principles of a rhetorical analysis:

- **Modes of Rhetoric (Logos, Pathos, Ethos):** Explain Aristotle's modes of rhetoric (see p. 181).
- **Techniques:** Students will consider how these appeals are developed through different techniques used by the author. Go over a few techniques with students (see p. 182). Note that language, positive and negative connotations, personification, repetition, and rhetorical questions are used.
- **Structure/Organization:** Students should consider where the appeals are placed within the documents and why they are there. They should also consider the overall structure of the document as it often supports the logos appeal (it helps the author's rationale "make sense" by putting ideas in this order). Why is it important that the points are placed structurally where they are? Throughout the analysis, the elements of logos, ethos, and pathos interact with structure, techniques, and point of view.

Step 3: Rhetorical Analysis Wheel: Separate Elements. Lead students through completing relevant parts of the Rhetorical Analysis Wheel. Students do not need to write detailed explanations on the organizer, just notes. Focus first on the separate elements.

- **Purpose:**
  - *What is President Roosevelt's purpose in delivering this message?* To persuade the American people to carry on toward progress by moving forward together.

- **Message/Claim:**
  - *What is Roosevelt's main claim? What is the main idea he is proving?* America will carry on toward progress by addressing the concerns of all.

- **Point of View/Assumptions:**
  - *What is Roosevelt's point of view toward progress? What are his assumptions?* FDR believes Americans should cautiously handle prosperity; it can distract Americans from progressing because of the self-interest involved. He assumes that government involvement into the affairs of people is welcomed, justified, and of goodwill.

- **Structure:**
  - *What is the overall structure of the speech?* Problem-solution.

- **Techniques:**
  - *What are some techniques you notice within the speech?* Rhetorical questions, personification, etc.

- **Logos:**
  - *What are the main points? How does the author support his claim with evidence and facts? What are the main "reasons" that support the claim?* **Logos/Reasoning:** FDR notes that America has progressed, but not arrived, and the American people should be warned by the disasters of prosperity. He lists positive state of affairs, lists negative state of affairs, and explains a hopeful future via government involvement. He provides evidence of a negative state of affairs ("I see millions . . . ").

- **Pathos:**
  - *What emotion(s) does the author attempt to evoke in the audience (pathos)?* FDR appeals to a sense of sympathy ("I see millions . . . ") and pride ("If I know aught of the will of our people . . . ").

- **Ethos:**
  - *Is the author credible? How does the author establish trust? Is evidence credible?* FDR is speaking at his Second Inaugural Address and acknowledges the progress made during his presidency. He also refers to the government as effective and competent to build trust. Evidence is not supported with specific credibility, and he is somewhat biased with his enthusiasm for the competency of the government in addressing problems.

- **Implications:**
  - *What are the short-term and long-term implications/consequences of this document?* This speech set the stage for many of FDR's initiatives. During his second term, Congress passed the Housing Act, laws were made to establish minimum wage (Fair Labor Standards Act), and over 3.3 million jobs were developed through WPA (Works Progress Administration).

Step 4: Combined elements for complexity. Combine elements to develop more complex questions. Students may draw arrows on their wheels to show how elements relate (pathos + techniques, etc.).

- **Logos/Techniques:**
  - *What techniques are used to develop the reasoning in his argument?* He sets up the first point by asking a rhetorical question ("Shall we pause now and turn our back . . . "), uses personification to introduce the idea that we should be warned by the disasters of prosperity ("Comfort says . . . timidity says . . . "), addresses a counterclaim and acknowledges that we have progressed ("true, we have come far . . . "), and explains how progress today is more difficult in light of prosperity.

- **Logos/Structure:**
  - *How is the argument structured logically?* Problem-solution. It is also organized inductively. His main claim is that Americans will carry on by addressing the concerns of all. He provides evidence first and then makes this claim.

- **Pathos/Techniques:**
  - *How does the author develop pathos appeals (techniques)?* He uses repetition ("I see millions . . . ") to develop sympathy. He develops a sense of urgency with "at this very moment . . . ." He uses loaded language (meager, indecent, poverty, denying work, ill-housed, ill-clad, ill-nourished) for sympathy and pride ("goodwill," "effective government," "uncorrupted by cancers of injustice," "strong," "will to peace," "long-cherished ideals").

- **Pathos/Structure:**
  - *Where does he place pathos appeals (structure)? Why? Do they change? Why?* The pathos appeals are in line with the problem-solution logos structure. As he develops the problem, he evokes sympathy. As he develops the solution, he evokes pride.

- **Ethos/Techniques/Structure:**
  - *What techniques are used to establish ethos appeals and why are they placed where they are?* He includes "we" and "us" throughout the speech to connect with the audience. As he uses "we" he establishes that he has been a part of the present gains. The "we" language shifts to "I"— revealing that the audience can really trust him since he himself sees the problems. He shifts again to "we" when connecting the audience to the goodwill of the nation.

- **Evaluation:**
  - *How effective is the author in supporting his claim? Is there a balance of pathos, ethos, and logos appeals? Is there too much bias or emotional manipulation? Is the claim fully supported?* President Roosevelt is effective in supporting the claim that America will continue on toward progress by addressing the concerns of all. There is a balance of logos, ethos, and pathos appeals. FDR gives sufficient evidence of the problem with the repeated "I see" statements, although the credibility of this evidence is not specific, but general.

SOCIAL STUDIES CONNECTIONS WHEEL INSTRUCTIONS

The Social Studies Connections Wheel is a visual tool that helps students make connections among social studies concepts. Students analyze cause-effect relationships, short- and long-term implications, the development of problems, and emergence of new ideas. This tool allows students to analyze a key idea, person, or event through a broader historical context rather than as an isolated entity. Essentially, the wheel shows how all the factors (e.g., economics, geography, world context, etc.) relate to each other and affect a historical idea. It also shows how the historical idea affects multiple factors (e.g., the printing press affected culture/religion, which influenced conflict among churches and governments).

Using the Social Studies Connection Wheel

Cause-effect relationships on the wheel work from the center outward, from the outward in, and across concepts. The inner wheel conceptually spins so that its elements interact with each other and the outer wheel to show the convergence of concepts. However, each factor can relate to another, regardless of its placement on the wheel. For example, economics affects social structure, geography affects economics, and scientific innovation affects culture.

The historical key idea, document, event, civilization, or person is placed in the inner circle. Students consider how multiple factors influenced the key idea and how the key idea influenced multiple factors. When two factors combine, a problem or new idea emerges from the interaction. For example, for the topic of Indian removal, government and geography interact to cause a problem (for American Indians) and a solution (for the U.S. government). Additional complexity is added when examining economic, cultural, and social factors that influenced a specific event or time period.

The Social Studies Connections Wheel Guide (Appendix B) shows specific prompts for each factor included on the wheel. The teacher may simply refer to the model during instruction or students may take notes on the Blank Social Studies Connection Wheel using arrows to show how the factors relate. Students may note the answers to the "basic" questions on the wheel and then discuss their interactions with other factors. Consider making a poster of the Social Studies Connections Wheel Guide to refer to throughout instruction. Once students are accustomed to using the wheel, encourage students to develop their own questions about the relationship between the various factors.

Students can make their own interactive paper-plate model of the wheel. Two different colored papers may be used for the inner and outer circles, secured with a brass paper fastener. Students may use the wheels as visuals in small groups.

Sample questions for Social Studies Connections Wheel. The following questions can be asked for analyzing a historical person, idea, event, or document. Note that complexity is added by combining concepts.

- **Basic questions:** Ask students to identify the factors from the wheel that are related to the historical key idea.
  - **Economics:** What is the economic situation? What are the main goods and services? What resources are available?
  - **World context:** What else is happening in the world at this time? What other movements are taking place?
  - **Politics/power:** What type of government is in place? What laws are relevant to this idea? Who is in power?
  - **Social structure:** What issues of equity do you notice? What were the needs of families during this time? How does education relate?
  - **Culture:** What religious values are relevant? What art, literature, or music relates to this topic?
  - **Geography:** Where do people move? How does the environment affect the people?
  - **Innovation:** What new technology has emerged? How has communication evolved? How does science relate to this topic?
  - **Conflict:** What problems are the people experiencing? What wars are relevant? What internal and political conflicts are happening?

- Sample questions that add complexity:
  - How did the geography of the South influence the development of power, trade, and culture? How did these factors influence slavery in the South?
  - How did the temperance movement and proabolitionism incite momentum for the Women's Suffrage Movement?
  - How does geography influence innovation for transportation, energy, communication, and basic needs?
  - How did two factors from the wheel interact to create conflict?
  - How did economic and political factors interact to cause conflict between the colonies and Britain?
  - What is the key problem and how does it relate to the current economic and geographic context?
  - What is the key problem regarding Indian removal, and how did multiple concepts interact to cause the problem?
  - How did multiple factors interact/converge to create a solution (or new idea)?
  - How did two factors interact to create the new ideas proposed in the Mayflower Compact?
  - What were the long-term implications of the Protestant Reformation on the economic structure of Europe and social class structure of America?
  - What were the implications of Indian removal on the geographic boundaries of states and social class for American Indians?

Applying the Social Studies Connections Wheel to primary sources. Include multiple social studies factors in questions pertaining to primary sources. Examples:
- What social studies factors from the wheel do you notice in the document? Explain the cause-effect relationship between these.
- What were the cultural, social, political, and economic implications/consequences of this primary source document?
- How might this document be viewed from an economic perspective? From an environmental perspective?
- What social studies factors converged to create a problem in the document?
- What social studies factors converged to develop or propose a new idea in the document?
- Change generates additional change. Relate this generalization to a social studies factor on the wheel and cite evidence from the primary source document.
- Where does the primary source document "fit" on the wheel? Why?
- What were the intended implications of this document? Explain by addressing at least two social studies ideas from the wheel.

Example Social Studies Connections Wheel Lesson

The sample content will be the Women's Suffrage Movement.

Step 1: Social studies content attainment. Read primary and secondary sources related to a topic of the Women's Suffrage Movement in the 1910s. Participate in class discussions, inquiry, and activities related to the content.

Step 2: Social studies connections—separate factors. Use the Social Studies Connections Wheel to ask basic questions for separate factors:

- **World context:** What other movements were happening in the world in the 1910s?
- **Innovation:** How did factory working conditions affect women during the Industrial Revolution?
- **Social structure:** What was the role of women in families during the 1910s? How might this have affected antisuffrage perspectives?
- **Conflict:** What wars were happening? What other conflicts were happening in the early 1900s?
- **Geography:** What was the first state to adopt women's suffrage?

Step 3: Social studies connections—combined elements for complexity. Use the Social Studies Connections Wheel to ask complex questions with combined factors listed on the wheel.

- What three factors converged to create an opportunity for the Women's Suffrage Movement to grow?
- How did World War I, industrialization, and proabolitionism influence the Women's Suffrage Movement?
- What were the long-term consequences of the 19th Amendment on politics, families, and culture?
- What factors were in conflict with each other to spur the Women's Suffrage Movement?

Step 4: Big Idea Reflection: Primary Sources. Provide content extension with a related primary source document. Use the Big Idea Reflection: Primary Sources in Appendix B as a guide. Have students view the image "Votes for Women Broadside" at http://www.loc.gov/item/rbcmiller002522 before answering the questions below.

- **Concepts:** What social studies factors do you notice in the image?
- **Relationships/interactions:** What problem is caused by the interaction of these factors?
- **Issue:** What is the author's point of view toward the issue? What assumptions are made?

- **Insight:** What insight does this document provide about the values and culture of the time period?
- **World/Community/Individual:** What questions does the author want individuals to consider?
- **Implications:** What is the message of this document, and what are the implications of this message on three social studies factors?

Appendix B

Blank Models and Guides

BLANK RHETORICAL ANALYSIS WHEEL

Directions: Draw arrows across elements to show connections.

Text: _____

Purpose/Context

Point of View

Logos

Techniques

Pathos

Claim

Ethos

Structure/
Organization

Implications

Evaluation

Created by Emily Mofield, Ed.D., & Tamra Stambaugh, Ph.D., 2015.

RHETORICAL ANALYSIS WHEEL GUIDE

Text: _____

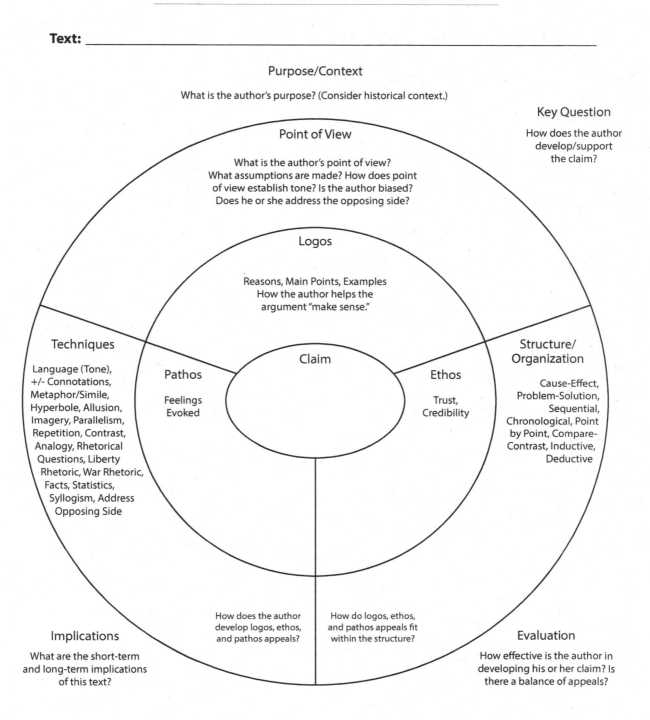

Purpose/Context

What is the author's purpose? (Consider historical context.)

Key Question

How does the author develop/support the claim?

Point of View

What is the author's point of view? What assumptions are made? How does point of view establish tone? Is the author biased? Does he or she address the opposing side?

Logos

Reasons, Main Points, Examples How the author helps the argument "make sense."

Techniques

Language (Tone), +/- Connotations, Metaphor/Simile, Hyperbole, Allusion, Imagery, Parallelism, Repetition, Contrast, Analogy, Rhetorical Questions, Liberty Rhetoric, War Rhetoric, Facts, Statistics, Syllogism, Address Opposing Side

Pathos

Feelings Evoked

Claim

Ethos

Trust, Credibility

Structure/ Organization

Cause-Effect, Problem-Solution, Sequential, Chronological, Point by Point, Compare-Contrast, Inductive, Deductive

Implications

What are the short-term and long-term implications of this text?

How does the author develop logos, ethos, and pathos appeals?

How do logos, ethos, and pathos appeals fit within the structure?

Evaluation

How effective is the author in developing his or her claim? Is there a balance of appeals?

Created by Emily Mofield, Ed.D., & Tamra Stambaugh, Ph.D., 2015.

BLANK TEXT ANALYSIS WHEEL

Directions: Draw arrows across elements to show connections.

Text: _____

Purpose/Context

Point of View

Point #1

Evidence

Techniques

Structure/
Organization

Point #2

Central Idea

Point #3

Evidence

Evidence

Implications

Evaluation

Created by Emily Mofield, Ed.D., & Tamra Stambaugh, Ph.D., 2015.

TEXT ANALYSIS WHEEL GUIDE

Text: _____

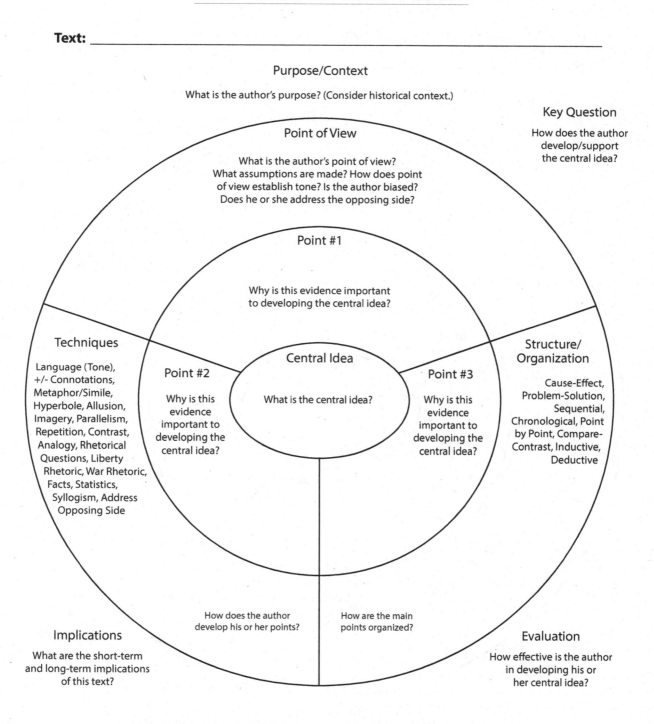

Purpose/Context

What is the author's purpose? (Consider historical context.)

Key Question

How does the author develop/support the central idea?

Point of View

What is the author's point of view? What assumptions are made? How does point of view establish tone? Is the author biased? Does he or she address the opposing side?

Point #1

Why is this evidence important to developing the central idea?

Techniques

Language (Tone), +/- Connotations, Metaphor/Simile, Hyperbole, Allusion, Imagery, Parallelism, Repetition, Contrast, Analogy, Rhetorical Questions, Liberty Rhetoric, War Rhetoric, Facts, Statistics, Syllogism, Address Opposing Side

Point #2

Why is this evidence important to developing the central idea?

Central Idea

What is the central idea?

Point #3

Why is this evidence important to developing the central idea?

Structure/ Organization

Cause-Effect, Problem-Solution, Sequential, Chronological, Point by Point, Compare-Contrast, Inductive, Deductive

How does the author develop his or her points?

How are the main points organized?

Implications

What are the short-term and long-term implications of this text?

Evaluation

How effective is the author in developing his or her central idea?

Created by Emily Mofield, Ed.D., & Tamra Stambaugh, Ph.D., 2015.

BLANK SOCIAL STUDIES CONNECTIONS WHEEL

Directions: Draw arrows across elements to show connections.

Text: _____

Context/Era

Economics

Innovation

Politics
and Power

Geography

Social
Structure

Conflicts

Historical
Key Idea

World Context

Culture

Implications
Consider how each of the factors interact to produce problems, solutions, and new ideas.

Created by Emily Mofield, Ed.D., & Tamra Stambaugh, Ph.D., 2015.

SOCIAL STUDIES CONNECTIONS WHEEL GUIDE

Text: _____

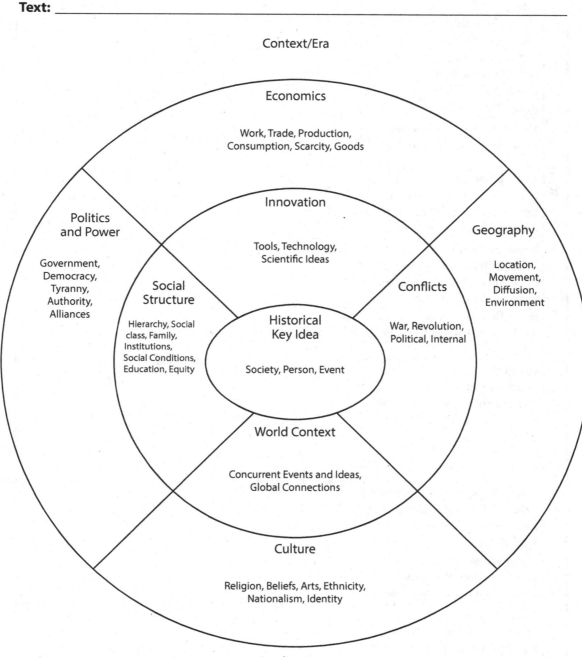

Context/Era

Economics

Work, Trade, Production,
Consumption, Scarcity, Goods

Innovation

Tools, Technology,
Scientific Ideas

Politics
and Power

Government,
Democracy,
Tyranny,
Authority,
Alliances

Geography

Location,
Movement,
Diffusion,
Environment

Social
Structure

Hierarchy, Social
class, Family,
Institutions,
Social Conditions,
Education, Equity

Conflicts

War, Revolution,
Political, Internal

Historical
Key Idea

Society, Person, Event

World Context

Concurrent Events and Ideas,
Global Connections

Culture

Religion, Beliefs, Arts, Ethnicity,
Nationalism, Identity

Implications
Consider how each of the factors interact to produce problems, solutions, and new ideas.

Created by Emily Mofield, Ed.D., & Tamra Stambaugh, Ph.D., 2015.

BIG IDEA REFLECTION: PRIMARY SOURCES

What?	**Concepts:** What social studies factors are related to this document (e.g., economics, geography, social structure, power/politics, conflict, culture, innovation, etc.)?	
	Relationships/Interactions: How are the social studies factors related in the document? What cause-effect relationships between each factor do you notice? How do their interactions cause problems or new ideas?	
	Issue/Problem: What is the main issue, problem, or conflict? Does the document pose a solution? What is the author's point of view/assumption toward the issue?	
So What?	**Insight:** What insight does this provide about the values and culture of the time period?	
	World/Community/Individual: How did this document relate to other world contexts? How did it impact specific communities/groups? What questions does the author want individuals to consider?	
Now What?	**Implications:** What action does the author want? What are the short- and long-term implications of this document and its message (consider multiple social studies factors)?	

REASONING ABOUT A SITUATION OR EVENT

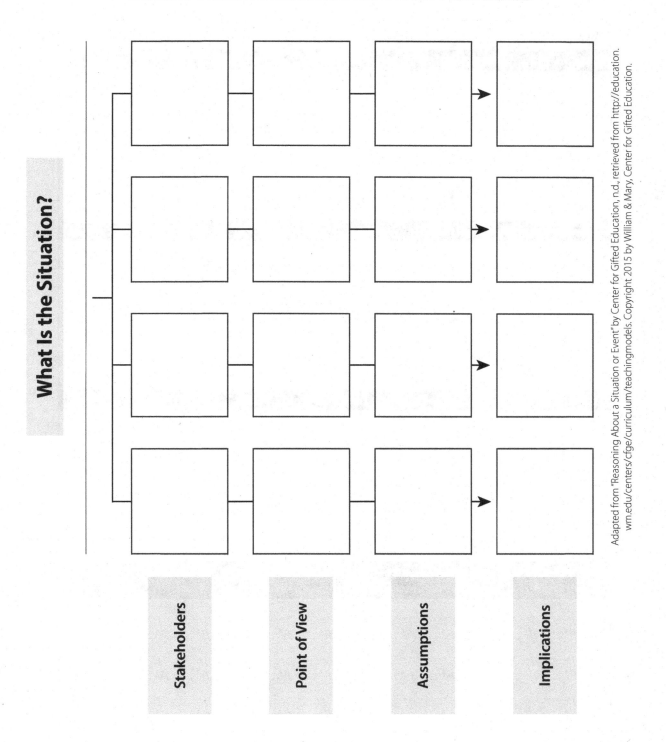

What Is the Situation?

Stakeholders

Point of View

Assumptions

Implications

Adapted from "Reasoning About a Situation or Event" by Center for Gifted Education, n.d., retrieved from http://education.wm.edu/centers/cfge/curriculum/teachingmodels. Copyright 2015 by William & Mary, Center for Gifted Education.

CONCEPT ORGANIZER

Text: _____	Text: _____	Text: _____
Freedom requires sacrifice.		
Freedom requires responsibility.		
Freedom is threatened by internal and external forces.		
Examine the relationship between freedom and another concept (e.g., security, power, conflict, change, order, unity, defense, fear, society, individual, etc.).		

FREEDOM CHART

Text: _____	Text: _____	Text: _____
How would this author define freedom and whom it's for?		
What is the reason we must achieve this freedom?		
By what means must it be achieved?		
What will be the implications for achieving the freedom?		

Appendix C

Rubrics

208

RUBRIC 1: PRODUCT RUBRIC

Name: _____ Date: _____ Lesson: _____

	Needs Improvement	Fair	Acceptable	Excellent
Completion	Not turned in or late.	Missing key pieces.	Completed but lacks thought and professionalism.	Satisfactorily meets all requirements and expectations of the task.
Content/ Concept	Limited or vague connection.	Little connection from lesson content is made to the freedom theme.	Accurately relates lesson content ideas of freedom to assignment.	Insightfully relates the theme of freedom to assignment.
Thinking	Limited or vague evidence.	Reasoning is inaccurate. Lacks originality, logical conclusions, or substantial claims.	Demonstrates some evidence of higher level thinking (creativity, evaluation, or analysis).	Demonstrates substantial evidence of higher level thinking (creativity, analysis, or evaluation with evidence).
Student-Developed Criteria				

Comments:

RUBRIC 2: CULMINATING PROJECT RUBRIC

Name: _____   Date: _____

	Needs Improvement	Fair	Acceptable	Excellent
Completion	Not turned in or late.	Missing key pieces.	Completed but lacks thought and professionalism.	Satisfactorily meets all requirements and expectations of the task.
Evidence	Limited or no evidence.	Little support or elaboration to support ideas and generalizations.	Gives support/elaboration to support ideas.	Gives meaningful support/elaboration to support ideas and generalizations.
Concept	Limited or vague connection.	Little connection from unit content is made to the big idea of freedom.	Accurately relates ideas of freedom to assignment.	Insightfully relates the big idea of freedom to assignment.
Content	Limited or no content application.	Vague connections to content are made.	Some connections to content are made with some evidence.	Synthesizes content across lessons with substantial support and evidence.
Process	Limited or vague evidence	Reasoning is inaccurate. Lacks originality, logical conclusions, or substantial claims.	Demonstrates some evidence of higher level thinking (i.e., creativity, evaluation, or analysis).	Provides insightful evidence to support higher level thinking (i.e., creativity, evaluation, or analysis) in developing complex conclusions.
Student-Developed Criteria				

Comments:

About the Authors

Emily Mofield, Ed.D., is the lead consulting teacher for gifted education for Sumner County Schools in Tennessee and is involved in supporting several projects with Vanderbilt Programs for Talented Youth. She has also taught as a gifted education language arts middle school teacher for 10 years. Her work is devoted to developing challenging differentiated curriculum for gifted learners and addressing their social/emotional needs. Emily regularly presents professional development on effective differentiation for advanced learners. She is a national board certified teacher in language arts and has been recognized as the Tennessee Association for Gifted Children Teacher of the Year.

Tamra Stambaugh, Ph.D., is an assistant research professor in special education and executive director of Programs for Talented Youth at Vanderbilt University Peabody College. She received her Ph.D. in Educational Policy, Planning, and Leadership with an emphasis in gifted education from William & Mary. She is the coauthor/editor of several books including *Serving Gifted Students in Rural Settings* (coedited with Susannah Wood), *Comprehensive Curriculum for Gifted Learners* (with Joyce VanTassel-Baska), *Overlooked Gems: A National Perspective on Low-Income Promising Students* (with Joyce VanTassel-Baska), *Leading Change in Gifted Education* (with Bronwyn MacFarlane), the *Jacob's Ladder Reading Comprehension Program Series* (with Joyce VanTassel-Baska), and *Practical Solutions for Underrepresented Gifted Students: Effective Curriculum* (with Kim Chandler), as well as numerous book chapters and research articles. Stambaugh's research interests focus on talent development support structures for gifted students and key curriculum and instructional interventions that support gifted learners—especially those students from rural backgrounds and those from poverty.

Common Core State Standards Alignment

Grade Level/Cluster	Common Core State Standards in ELA/Literacy
Grades 9–10: Reading Informational Text	RI.9-10.1 Cite strong and thorough textual evidence to support analysis of what the text says explicitly as well as inferences drawn from the text.
	RI.9-10.2 Determine a central idea of a text and analyze its development over the course of the text, including how it emerges and is shaped and refined by specific details; provide an objective summary of the text.
	RI.9-10.3 Analyze how the author unfolds an analysis or series of ideas or events, including the order in which the points are made, how they are introduced and developed, and the connections that are drawn between them.
	RI.9-10.4 Determine the meaning of words and phrases as they are used in a text, including figurative, connotative, and technical meanings; analyze the cumulative impact of specific word choices on meaning and tone (e.g., how the language of a court opinion differs from that of a newspaper).
	RI.9-10.5 Analyze in detail how an author's ideas or claims are developed and refined by particular sentences, paragraphs, or larger portions of a text (e.g., a section or chapter).
	RI.9-10.6 Determine an author's point of view or purpose in a text and analyze how an author uses rhetoric to advance that point of view or purpose.
Grades 9–10: Speaking and Listening	SL.9-10.1 Initiate and participate effectively in a range of collaborative discussions (one-on-one, in groups, and teacher-led) with diverse partners on grades 9–10 topics, texts, and issues, building on others' ideas and expressing their own clearly and persuasively.

Grade Level/Cluster	Common Core State Standards in ELA/Literacy
Grades 9–10: Speaking and Listening, *continued*	SL.9-10.1c Propel conversations by posing and responding to questions that relate the current discussion to broader themes or larger ideas; actively incorporate others into the discussion; and clarify, verify, or challenge ideas and conclusions.
	SL.9-10.1d Respond thoughtfully to diverse perspectives, summarize points of agreement and disagreement, and, when warranted, qualify or justify their own views and understanding and make new connections in light of the evidence and reasoning presented.
Grades 9–10: Literacy in History and Social Studies	RH.9-10.1 Cite specific textual evidence to support analysis of primary and secondary sources, attending to such features as the date and origin of the information.
	RH.9-10.2 Determine the central ideas or information of a primary or secondary source; provide an accurate summary of how key events or ideas develop over the course of the text.
	RH.9-10.3 Analyze in detail a series of events described in a text; determine whether earlier events caused later ones or simply preceded them.
	RH.9-10.4 Determine the meaning of words and phrases as they are used in a text, including vocabulary describing political, social, or economic aspects of history/social science.
	RH.9-10.5 Analyze how a text uses structure to emphasize key points or advance an explanation or analysis.
	RH.9-10.8 Assess the extent to which the reasoning and evidence in a text support the author's claims.
	RH.9-10.9 Compare and contrast treatments of the same topic in several primary and secondary sources.
Grades 9–10: Writing	W.9-10.1 Write arguments to support claims in an analysis of substantive topics or texts, using valid reasoning and relevant and sufficient evidence.
	W.9-10.4 Produce clear and coherent writing in which the development, organization, and style are appropriate to task, purpose, and audience.
	W.9-10.9 Draw evidence from literary or informational texts to support analysis, reflection, and research.
	W.9-10.10 Write routinely over extended time frames (time for research, reflection, and revision) and shorter time frames (a single sitting or a day or two) for a range of tasks, purposes, and audiences.